the
existential
experience

the
existential
experience

RALPH HARPER

the johns hopkins university press

baltimore and london

Frontispiece: sculpture by Reg Butler, from the collection of
Mrs. Alan Wurtzberger. Photo Peter Winants.

The Johns Hopkins University Press, Baltimore, Maryland 21218
The Johns Hopkins University Press Ltd., London

Library of Congress Catalog Card Number 72–4009
ISBN 0-8018-1409-X (clothbound edition)
ISBN 0-8018-1423-5 (paperback edition)

Originally published, 1972
Johns Hopkins Paperbacks edition, 1972

Library of Congress Cataloging in Publication data will
be found on the last printed page of this book.

contents

preface

My first book, *Existentialism: A Theory of Man*, was published in 1948. I have often thought of revising it but have found it impossible. I no longer have a theory of man, in the sense that the "interiorized scholasticism" of that book represented such a theory, and I now know much more about the interior life and the existential tradition than I then did. I would have to start all over, or almost.

Why write another book on existentialism anyway, since there are already so many, too many? Simply because I have never been satisfied with the others I have read. But I have been reluctant to write another for a second reason. Dr. Laing says of himself, "I am a specialist, God help me, in events in inner space and time."[1] When I read that, I am reminded that I have come to think of myself as a specialist too, in the themes of interior experience, as understood by an existential philosopher, a theologian, a poet. And yet I am embarrassed to say so publicly, even though anyone who has been working over existential themes for thirty-seven years might turn in some kind of claim, if only for singlemindedness.

I now know too much to be sure of any objective coherence that the mind has any right to — and too little to suit my own philosophical ideals. I know how diverse and complex — and above all, elusive — are the experiential sources of existential thought. I would not even dream of trying now to compose a theory of existential dynamics, or an "existential syntax," as I put it long ago. However little I could ever satisfy the stringency of Wittgenstein, I am sufficiently inhibited by recollections of my own inner life not to demand more of myself than I can deliver. And so I have no illusions about adequacy or completeness.

I have come to the point where I feel I can do little more — and perhaps that is enough — than write about a few major themes which are related one to the other, categories of experience that I know at first hand. The following pages are written in the hope that they may arouse a tremor of recognition on the part of other specialists in the interior life. Like Kafka, I would say that the thought of my task never leaves me, and I suppress everything that might get in the way of carrying it out.[2] And that task is never done.

The task is nothing less than the whole shape of the inner life of man. Monstrous! Yes, quite impossible. And yet, as Camus has counseled, "Nothing is true that forces one to exclude."[3] Of course, any theory does this, and however drawn I have been to a succession of other people's constructs, I now shy at the temptation to present another of my own. A selection of themes is presumptuous enough, implying some commitment to structure. Theory by the back door? Possibly. All I know is that in the years since 1934, all the categories of interior experience — my own and those of my masters — have always seemed to fall of their own accord into a few large areas of focus. The argument of this book, a very simple one, is that by looking at five of these areas, one can begin to see the whole of the inner experience of human existence.

Even so, however objective the themes are, there are always people who say, "But what is all the fuss about?" There is only one good reply to that, and St. Augustine gave it: "Give me one that longs, give me one that hungers, give me one that is wandering in this wilderness and thirsting and panting for the fountain of his eternal home; give me such an one, and he will know what I would say."[4] The world of the seeker and lover is filled with passion and commitment, and he not only sees everything with new eyes, he understands himself with immediacy and intense clarity. He knows who he is and what he wants; he knows also the limitations of both freedom and desire. So the existentialist, once awakened to the claims of his existence, will never be satisfied until he is liberated from the fears and nightmares of rejection and allowed to live in a world where he knows what it is to live in the present.

No one is more aware than I of the limitations of existentialist language, its ambiguity, and the dangers of emotional rhetoric. I would welcome more clarity without exhortation, if I really thought it possible to suggest in any other way the spaciousness and urgency that belong to the interior life. We cannot and should not discard metaphorical language here any more than in poetry or mystical theology. And yet we have no right to boast, as Kierkegaard did, that we are able to set out "the decisive qualifications of the whole compass of existence"[5] in this or any other way. All we have a right to say is something like "Look here, look there. See what really happens."

Much has been made by some European philosophers of what is called the phenomenological method. I do not think this is very important to existentialism. What Heidegger and Sartre have left us could have been both thought and said by them had they known nothing of Husserl's method. Their principal themes, their insights, structures, and visions, seem to me to be accessible enough without that method because they are parts of a much broader philosophical and theological heritage. For one thing they had both read Kierkegaard and Nietzsche and, in the case of Sartre, Heidegger. A student of Augustine has no trouble understanding them or their precursors without the help of Husserl's phenomenology.

A certain kind of mind — a certain kind of philosopher — feels safer with a method or a theory. But if one is lucky, he finds that life does not fit into theoretical frames. The older I grow the more I come to respect the way experience forces me to review and revise. Impatient with other people's theories, I am constantly being disenchanted by my own. In a sense I am back where I started, on the first page of my first book, with what I called, after Unamuno, the man of flesh and bone, but now I prefer to speak of the man of dreams and nightmares, absences and presences. The real change, apart from the usual one of accumulation and refinement, has been that I am more confident now, less dependent on nostalgia. I know that the unexpected does happen.

7. Sept. 75

the
existential
experience

interior
experience

THE EXISTENTIAL TRADITION

There is no easily defined theory of experience which can be identified as existentialism. There are only existentialists. The first thing to learn about existentialism is that there are certain philosophers, theologians, and novelists to get to know well: Kierkegaard, Pascal, St. Augustine, then Nietzsche, Dostoevsky, and Kafka, then Jaspers, Heidegger, Barth, Buber, Marcel, Tillich, Sartre, and Camus. If you know their writings thoroughly you will know the major and minor themes of the interior life thoroughly, as seen through the eyes of descriptive reflection. It has been said of St. Augustine that he was the first modern man; it could be said of Pascal that he was the second. The existentialists of the nineteenth and twentieth centuries have fulfilled the destinies of these precursors.

The twentieth-century existentialists were brought up on the nineteenth, fortified by Augustine and Pascal. They continually betray their inheritance and usually acknowledge their predecessors. From our point of view they are a series of thinkers who respected each other. And yet Augustine, Pascal, Kierkegaard, Dostoevsky, Nietzsche — and, to a lesser degree, Kafka, Unamuno, Proust — were in fact all isolated thinkers, genuine originators, who owed little to each other. But one cannot imagine Jaspers and Heidegger without Kierkegaard and Nietzsche, Sartre without Heidegger, Camus without Nietzsche and Kafka. It was once possible to think and write to a great degree outside the context of one's predecessors, although, as in the case of Kierkegaard and Hegel, one might be reacting to the ideas of one of them. In the present century, even the strongest minds have grown from the soil of other great minds of their own and earlier times. One should not, therefore, expect, if one wants to think deeply and well, to be original in the same way that Kierkegaard and Nietzsche were. They were authentic isolates; we cannot be, and do not need to be.

Both Kierkegaard and Nietzsche thought they had said the last word. Nietzsche's "last word" is arguable, but it is a fully developed statement. His major contribution — his understanding of a new event in cultural history, the spiritual nihilism of the "death of God" — is a challenge the consequences of which still have not been completely accepted or understood. As for Kierkegaard, although he has been called the father of existentialism, it is his sons — Jaspers, Heidegger, and others who have fleshed out what he had only outlined.

This is the place to point out that none of these men set out to be "existentialists." In fact, both Heidegger and Camus have tried to dissociate themselves from existentialism, probably because they did not want to be appraised in the same terms as Jaspers and Sartre. To call oneself an existentialist in no way detracts from whatever else one is. One should be proud to be able to add something to the tradition. How else can one be unique, or original, but by placing one's own contribution to human understanding alongside someone else's? It is prudent to be wary of being identified with another man's perspective, but it should nevertheless be possible for a controlled mind to understand a particular vision — Sartre's, for example — without accepting it.

Each of the major writers in the tradition set out to do something other than to name and define the major existential themes (or as Kierkegaard put it, "the decisive qualifications of the whole compass of existence"). Kierkegaard, for example, intended to "reintroduce Christianity into Christendom,"[1] and if he wrote about human existence in a new way it was because he was convinced that Christians had forgotten what it means to exist. Nietzsche had what he would call a nose for theological putrefaction and busied himself with its causes and consequences. But he never arranged in any order, any more than Kierkegaard had, the major themes of interior experience. They both singled out problems that were important to them. It is only now that we are in a position to piece together the whole puzzle and see something like a whole.

As for Jaspers, to whom academic existentialism owes so much, he himself saw his existential thinking as a preparation for a new look at metaphysics. Heidegger's major work, *Being and Time*, from which both theologians and psychiatrists have borrowed so extensively, was intended to be a preparatory study for a new approach to the problem of Being. If we call these men existential philosophers, it is not because they set out toward the same city but rather because they had to stop by at that city on their way elsewhere.

5 § interior experience

THE PHILOSOPHICAL IMAGINATION

Although it is correct to think of existentialists primarily as philosophers and theologians, it is common knowledge today that the themes they develop are most vividly illustrated in literature and the visual arts. Indeed, Dostoevsky, Kafka, Proust are sources for existential thinking as much as the professional philosophers, and except for strictly academic philosophers like Jaspers and Heidegger, almost all the other philosophers have written fiction and poetry as well. Kierkegaard and Nietzsche, in fact, would have been flattered to be known as artists. And so they were.

This is not accidental. However hard one may try to set apart existential thinking, as a philosophy, by calling it descriptive rather than analytical, it is clear that it is as metaphorical as poetry itself, while at the same time its analyses of data, and its metaphors, can be stretched as far as the individual existentialist can go. The interior experience of any man, as he knows it, is largely emotional, and the world of feeling does not yield itself easily to precise linguistic definition or analysis. For this reason it would be wise to think of existential thinking always as exploratory and provisional, however intensely it is felt and however carefully and clearly it appears to be organized. It is primarily suggestive rather than definitive and therefore by nature is closer to art than to science. If reflection gives it the appearance of science at times, one should treat that appearance as one does any scientific hypothesis that needs experiment and trial before it can be pronounced upon.

Camus once said, "If you want to be a philosopher, write novels."[2] He himself did, but it is questionable whether his novels say anything that his essays did not or could not have said. I learned long ago that the themes of existential philosophers are also the themes and categories of thrillers, as I have attempted to demonstrate in a recent book, and it would also be relatively easy to prove the existentiality of American poetry of the last twenty years, and so on. I have known that the reason for the great interest today in tragedy, both classical and absurdist, is that we live in a time of intense interior reflection on the violent and inescapable contingencies of life. In this area we cannot afford to be shut off from the professional thinking of anyone, whether theologian, psychoanalyst, playwright, novelist, or filmmaker. They have many themes in common, but their treatments are different.

EXISTENTIAL THINKING

Twenty years ago I proposed a general education course at Harvard on homelessness but was told that this was a "marginal" subject. If I had been proposing a course in the related fields of history, sociology, and political science with such a topic, it might have been acceptable; no one could forget easily at that time the homelessness of millions of Europeans during and after World War II. But we were still not used to associating these causes of emotional homelessness with those experienced in America itself through the changes in spirituality that have affected comfortable, educated people. We had political and psychiatric categories for homelessness, and that was that. What I had in mind, however, was a study that would include themes like anonymity, recognition, loneliness, despair, identity, and depression, which could be described and discussed in both literary and philosophical terms. What I learned was that "interior experience" was not thought of as a valid dimension of experience because there was no existing discipline to handle it.

We still have, in this country, no accepted genre for philosophical meditation of the kind practiced so magnificently by Camus. Interior experience is chopped up into pieces that can then be called psychology, poetry, or mysticism. The indifference of academic philosophy has prevented such a new genre from appearing. And to make matters worse, existentialism, the only sustained effort to discuss interior experience in philosophical language, is expounded almost exclusively by non-existentialists, who, even when they are not hostile, cannot speak from personal experience. It is no wonder that whatever impression of a structured understanding of interior experience — existential experience — we do have usually fails to combine the major insights of the tradition and the first-hand experience of the essayist. Only an insider can find his way confidently through the weeds and thistles of the garden of the existentialist inheritance.

We have to begin with a simple objective, that of naming the major themes of that area of the interior experience which existentialism has cultivated. This could serve as a basis for the identification of those themes which are peculiarly American. We are, I believe, more concerned than our contemporaries in Europe with problems of identity. Camus, to say nothing of Kierkegaard, spent much time as a young man wondering what to do with his life and talents. But this is a problem of vocation, not identity. Identity is a function, so to speak, of essential loneliness, and we worry about it if we cannot tolerate spiritual isolation. It is one thing to say "I know who I am, all right, but I don't know yet what to do with my life or whether what I do will be appreciated," and another to say "I can't stand living in a world which does not tell me I am wanted." The latter is also to be distinguished from the position of someone like K. in Kafka's *The Castle*, who wanted to be told he could stay in the village but who never despaired because he was not told. To feel the problem of identity in its acutest and purest form is to feel close to despair. Neither Kafka nor Camus questioned his identity, however much Kafka, for one, suffered under the tyranny of his father. Kafka's case is not a borderline case so much as it is one that emphasizes all the more intensely the difference between a man who does not know who he is until he is told and a man who knows, and then goes about his business, whether it is in battling the non-recognition of others or finding out where to use his talents.

It seems to me that when we speak of insecurity, we often have the shakiness of anonymity in mind rather than the risks implied in the contingencies of life. And so I see a difference between the increasingly common incidence of clinical depression in psychotherapy and the state of despair that Kierkegaard and Tillich examine, a difference almost as great as that between dread (*angst*) and fear (*furcht*). Heidegger is helpful here: he distinguishes between a reaction to the indefinite and a reaction to something quite definite. This is why depression is harder to lighten.

I do not mean by this cursory observation that Americans are untouched by traditional existentialist categories or that this new terminology cannot be made to seem relevant. On the contrary, those who have not read a single book about existentialism quite casually, and correctly, refer to "existential situations" and "existential guilt." Enough has happened in the twentieth century to persuade educated men and women that there are situations and there are existential situations, those that shake a person to the core. And existential guilt imposes a burden that no reparation can erase. In truth, "existential thinking offers no security, no home for the homeless."[3]

AN INDIVIDUAL AND THE TRADITION

An outsider's questions to an existentialist should be "What do you find when you think about yourself, what is going on inside you, what are your primary immediate experiences?" And the existentialist as insider would reply, "You may well ask, for every time I look I find something different." We should know best that being that each of us is, and yet it is precisely what is most characteristic of us that we may not know at all. Yet who would deny the metaphor of an inner space, with its intentions, thoughts, feelings, crises, rhythms, order, surprises, events, and situations? Is existence itself an experience, or is one's approach to his existence through experiences? To follow through Kierkegaard's question about what it means to exist, we would have to think about what we are doing, apart from talking or using our bodies in other ways, such as writing, eating, walking, or performing other physical activities. To say "apart from" these external and physical actions is to rope off what it is meant by the interior. The themes and categories of this interior are types of intentionality, like despair or choice, states of mind, like failure or loneliness, stages of development of life, like death or presence, and, finally, the more abstract characterizations of existence as contingent and tragic.

Having lived over half a century now, with a professional interest in the content of minds, I have discovered how difficult it is to summarize the identifying marks of one's own thinking. It is relatively easy to do so for someone else, I found, particularly when one had books as evidence, and I supposed I could do the same for myself by rereading my own books (an otherwise trying occupation). Just as Camus' perspective on his experience involved the dualisms of the absurd and happiness, revolt and love, for me the nostalgic and the tragic were inseparable, or to put it in the terms of late middle age, they were the experiences of depression and insecurity. Where Camus was simply skeptical, I was more apt to be disillusioned. The difference is important; I think I expected more than he.

I do not think I have misrepresented myself or Camus. It is not hard to come up with characterizations that are simplistic and at the same time true. When one asks, "What goes on inside you?" there are two other kinds of answers that are harder to find. There are many themes and categories of experience that all have in common, and there are memories, associations, obsessions, nightmares, dreams, the web of sensibility that makes up the inner personality of each of us. This web is so close to us, so much a part of every moment and every level of consciousness, that no one should be surprised to find that in this way he does not know himself at all. This is why Proust's exploration in his long novel is so important to the history of existentialism. Apart from his special theories about the interior life, particularly regarding memory and time, he has demonstrated the infinite complexity and fullness of an inner registration of experience — the places and people, what they did, said, and felt. It is much easier to write a treatise on the major and minor themes of interior experience than to recover the total content of life once it has been lived. And yet each of us has such a content and is identified by it.

11 § interior experience

KALEIDOSCOPE OF THEMES

It is easy to list the most common existential themes and categories — as easy as listing the names of prominent existential philosophers — but it is not as useful. Go to them and read their books. Name the themes, and you still do not know what to do with them, unless you have some sort of context to put them in. That is the problem facing everyone who tries to write about existentialism, and the usual ways of solving it are either to attach these themes to the structure of some philosopher or to impose on them an order of one's own. Both solutions are unsatisfactory. There is no linear progression from one theme to another. You can start anywhere and you will end everywhere. One theme leads to all the rest. Associations of categories are both multiple and changing. Concentrate, as if in mystical contemplation, on the phenomenon of disquietude. Not only will you be able to compare it with other emotional symptoms, like restlessness, insecurity, anxiety, care, fear, dread, but you will also be in a better position to reflect on the nature of suffering, fate, freedom, death.

No wonder teachers and writers look for readymade approaches, such as the study of a book or an author. It seems the best way to maintain some kind of balance, to avoid the temptation to skip from one theme to another and another. It is a dizzying experience, and dizziness is not a state friendly to philosophy: it leads to superficiality or despair, rather than clarity. Nevertheless, I believe that there are a few areas of interior experience that one can focus on and that, as one moves one's eye from one to the other, one can achieve a fuller understanding of the nature of man. I also believe that this is done best when one moves in a certain order, from the simplest and most inescapable intuitions of self to the more elusive and yet more desirable experiences.

Does this undermine my skepticism about an existential system? Kierkegaard insisted, and I agree with him, that a logical system is possible but that an existential system is not. Certainly if one means by "system" an unalterable structure of categories, then there is no existential system. But if one imagines the interior life not as linear but as a building of blocks, not even as a mobile but as a toy kaleidoscope's constantly changing pattern made up of a finite number of elements related to each other in a finite number of ways, and if one imagines playing with five such kaleidoscopes, each having the same number of fragments but of slightly different shades, one might be able to see how, in moving from one major theme to another, the vision of the self both expands and deepens. Perhaps the analogy is not good enough, although it has the advantage of associating the mind's experience of elements and structure with an ever-shifting vision of what goes on inside it.

The themes of the existentialists are interlocking — the following pages will show that, if nothing else — not because the mind of man is a living organism, but because this organism is always in process. One ought to begin with the simpler intuitions of existence and move on to a consideration of the telltale uneasiness that is a basic note, a *cantus firmus* — the feeling of disquietude, the state of insecurity. Moving on to a consideration of the various causes of the void within the insecurity, one inevitably comes up against the most absolute void of all, the death of God. When we then reflect on the consequences, historical and psychological, of this night of absolutes, we find we are offered alternatives, as far apart as the extremes of self divided against self and self in harmony with self and others. Whether one is focusing on one of these areas or the other, the same several dozen themes weave in and out, to be seen each time in a different aspect or relation.

13 § interior experience

The five major themes — existence, insecurity, the void, self-isolation, presence — are themselves experiences that five words cannot adequately suggest. To say "existence" or "presence" is to recall two ultimate kinds of intuitive experience possible to all men to some degree, each with its vision and its mystery: the one a sense of self with self, the other of self with others. And yet even within or underneath the undistracted intuition, there is always the memory, if not the threat, of absence, separation, conflict.

The second, third, and fourth themes are themselves themes of conflict, so it should not be surprising that existentialism is usually remembered in terms of estrangement rather than of reconciliation. Perhaps life should be based on an intuition of identity, dreams of innocence, and presence. It is always lived under a threatening cloud of necessity, division, absence, isolation. The intuitive moments are of prime importance, but they are rare. Without a special intuition of self, one cannot be fully a person. But these flashes and moments do not color the surface of consciousness, as does *insecuritas*, for *insecuritas* constantly underlies consciousness and is inescapable, unlike the fear of a spiritual vacuum, which can remain submerged. If there is God, and we do not know him, then the cultural fact is not his absence but rather our lack of awareness. In the twentieth century, whether as absence or lack of awareness, the death of God, the menace of a spiritual vacuum, must be added to death and guilt as a cause of insecurity.

Nietzsche, whose obsession with the death of God was so overwhelming, never got much further than a simplistic fantasy of some of the consequences of His disappearance. He could have learned much from Dostoevsky. Indeed, we are now in a better position than either Dostoevsky or Nietzsche to outline the principal dark options open to a person who is preoccupied with total estrangement and not ready for or given the grace of presence. It is paradoxical that the darker the inner world looks after reflection on this fourth theme, the more appealing is the experience and light of presence that division and darkness suggest. But, as we have ruefully found out since Socrates, a vision is one thing, a new life another.

Perhaps, after all, there is something that binds all five themes together, some feature of ourselves that appears first as contingency, turns threatening, and finally can be converted into a sense of the infinite. I would call it the state of being unfinished, for our experience, which is unfinished as long as we are alive, is always shifting and changing, being assaulted and assisted, refusing and being refused, welcoming and being welcomed. It is this vitality which justifies the image of the kaleidoscope. Everything is there, and we have a right to expect the unexpected.

the
major themes

1 EXISTENCE

INTUITION

There is a kind of logical sense in mentioning existence first. Even if Kierkegaard exaggerated somewhat when he said that "all essential knowledge is related to existence"[1] — and he meant interior human existence — it is the preoccupation with this existence that makes possible the explorations of the more accessible portions of interior life. The more we take anything for granted, the less we think about it. And if a thing happens to be something of paramount importance, we may never get around to it or take the trouble to understand it. This would be a serious mistake, as anyone who has tried to explain existentialism to a class of students discovers. There are always those who cannot understand why one should spend the time thinking about the interior life (so "self-centered"), for normal persons, like themselves, do not have to do so. Their contempt provokes impatience. It is equally difficult for us to understand why questions of disquietude, death of God, divided self, and presence are not as important to others as they are to us. We are tempted to hypothesize two kinds of human beings, "them" and "us," those for whom existence is the central fact and question and those who are content to take everything for granted.[2]

Religious contemplatives have left a more intense and concrete record of their love for God than lovers of men and women (who may be more inhibited or less analytical). Likewise, existentially awakened persons have left surprisingly few and undeveloped accounts of the impact that their intuitions of existence have made on them. First things first: existence does precede everything else, and yet how can one speak of existence without speaking of this or that existing life? Indeed, existence is not only the first fact, it is both simple and complex: simple because undefinable, if not ineffable; complex because it is the deposit for everything else, both security and insecurity, depending on the vantage point of the intuition of existence. It may be that some people never look at themselves from any vantage point but that of other people on the outside, and we should not expect them to understand this most peculiarly personal of all experiences, the experience of the self. What is really hard to understand is that existentialist philosophers have, on the whole, given such partial and cursory attention to it. For this reason alone there is an advantage in having a tradition to draw upon. We can see how foolish it would be if we learned about existentialism from one existentialist only, say, Heidegger or Sartre, or even Kierkegaard. And if we had to depend on philosophers there would still be much that is essential which would not be told and which can be taught us by theologians, novelists, poets.

Some years ago Jacques Maritain wrote that although anguish may be found in the philosopher himself, it should be kept out of his philosophy. His condemnation of existentialism — for that is what he meant it to be — is shared by most non-existentialist philosophers, yet even Maritain claimed to be some kind of existentialist, holding that philosophy has to begin with an intuition of being. This too would be denied by many today. There is no doubt that anguish is kept out of most philosophy, but perhaps at a price that is not worth paying, the price of rejecting and excluding a quality of being which every man knows at first hand. The being of a man pleads to be understood, and that is what existentialism is all about.

For a long time — even in our own time — existential philosophers had to take great care to separate their analyses of the human condition from an inherited religious context. The history of existentialism is, in fact, closely associated with the history of theological doubt in modern times, thus our use of St. Augustine, Pascal, and Kierkegaard, as well as our encounters with Dostoevsky, Nietzsche, Freud, and Kafka. It is as though man has become an ultimate question to himself only when he is no longer assured of being in the mind and hands of God. Even that most highly individuated and mysterious classical man Socrates does not seem to us as concerned about his nature and destiny as about problems of knowledge and justice. Perhaps this is because we know him through Plato's eyes. But when we compare the results of his maxim, "know yourself," with Pascal's and Kierkegaard's repetition of it, we must contrast Socrates' imperturbability with their anguish and suspect that Socrates had something different in mind.

PRIORITY

Life does not begin with formulas, but we expect philosophy to do so. Heidegger knew he was reversing the traditional Western view of the relationship between essence and existence when he said that "the essence of man lies in his existence,"[3] that existence is prior to essence. Sartre seems to echo his teacher's words when he says that "existence precedes essence."[4] To most philosophers, essence comes first, for philosophers are men concerned with ideas, abstractions from existing realities, so much so that many of them are now willing to reduce philosophy to an examination of words and ideas, with little or no reference to reality. It is no wonder that linguistic analysts often use trivial examples and are hostile to those who insist that some experiences are so important that we cannot afford to wait until their descendants have clarified the major problems of discourse and meaning — if, indeed, it is possible to achieve such a goal in an experiential vacuum.

If all we could say about our existence as human beings is that we are, and that, like everything else we experience, we some day will cease to be, it would be impossible to convince anyone that the word "existence" is worth bothering about. The metaphysician has convinced himself that the only other philosophical question about existence is an impossible one, i.e., the definition of individual existence, and so with regret or impatience he waves this problem away too. This is why both Jaspers and Heidegger made such a point of using the German *Existenz* instead of the Latin *existentia*. They wanted to call attention to a third meaning of existence, one that justifies Heidegger's and Sartre's pat formulas. For them the question of existence is not only whether to be or not to be, but rather whether to be oneself or not be oneself. This may sound like saying the same thing in different words, or saying something nonsensical. Of course, there is an obvious sense in which one cannot be other than what one is — one's identity guarantees that. But it is just as obvious that because our ideas and even personalities change as we grow older, we do have apparent alternative ways of behaving. An accumulation of changes of one sort or another adds up often to a transformation of self.

It probably depends on what you have known about others or experienced directly. Most people, even intelligent people, do not seem to change very much. Conversions do not occupy the forefront of their concerns. It may be that only a generally non-religious age would find it easy to escape first-hand acquaintance with the changes that have always been central to religious experience. Indeed, Socrates' philosophical mission in life was to turn men around; unfortunately for him, not enough were turned around in time. He was the first philosopher to insist that a man was not a man if he did not learn to do his own thinking and to live by it. This is part of what Heidegger means by living authentically.

URGENCY ↤ Choice

To begin properly, existentially rather than intellectually, we should begin with those self-filled men St. Augustine, Pascal, and Kierkegaard. The first asks — rhetorically, to be sure — "What is nearer to me than myself?" Nothing, of course, and yet many men know much less about themselves, it seems, than about other beings. Pascal's bewilderment and impatience with those who cannot understand how urgent and ultimate are the questions about human destiny complements the apparent detachment of Augustine's observation. When we read Kierkegaard, who had himself read with immediate recognition both Augustine and Pascal, we see the beginnings of a new definition of existence. Curiously, he does not record what, for want of a better term, one might call the logically first approach, intuitions of self, at least not in so many words. To Kierkegaard existence involved isolation of self and choice of self. One can go a long way toward understanding the entire Kierkegaardian corpus if one sees it through these two categories: self-isolation and choice. But to simplify, Kierkegaard's own choice was self-isolation.

The young man who stood "like a lonely pine tree egotistically shut off, pointing to the skies and casting no shadow"[5] became the mature and sophisticated religious thinker who clutched his self-isolation to his breast: "No, no, my self-isolation cannot be broken, at least not now. The thought of breaking it occupies me so much, and at all times, that it only becomes more and more firmly embedded. . . . I must bear my punishment all my life, of remaining in the painful prison of my isolation."[6] A man of masks, a man whose registration of the traffic of his inner life was both infinite and exact, Kierkegaard presented the Pascalian and Augustinian obsession with one's work and destiny with a clarity and force that links him to Socrates at one end of the spectrum and to us at the other. "What I really lack is to be clear in my mind what I am to do, not what I am to know. . . . The thing is to understand myself, to see what God really wishes me to do; the thing is to find a truth which is true for me, to find the idea for which I can live and die."[7] He soon found that idea, the reintroduction of Christianity into Christendom by way of laying out the whole compass of existence. It is ironical that he had more luck with his goal than with his method. He died thinking that he had failed, but it was to his religious writings that Karl Barth and others turned when they needed help in recovering Christian biblical orthodoxy. While Barth and other theologians used Kierkegaard as inspiration, without surpassing him on essential points of doctrine, Karl Jaspers built on the Kierkegaardian program the first floor of the building called existentialism. Heidegger came along to put up the walls.

For Kierkegaard existence has to be understood in terms of choice, the most fundamental choice of what to do with one's life, what kind of being to make of oneself. It is this insight that Jaspers, Heidegger, and Sartre directly inherited. "I exist or I do not exist," said Jaspers, "but my *Existenz* as a possibility takes a step toward being or away from being, toward nothingness in every choice or decision I make;"[8] "*Existenz* warns me to detach myself from the world lest I become its prey;"[9] "I am possible *Existenz* in existence."[10] Here is the plainest distinction between the two terms. "The possibility of *Existenz* is what I live by; it is only in its realization that I am myself;"[11] "man is nothing else but what he makes of himself" (Sartre);[12] or, as Heidegger put it more metaphorically, man can win or lose himself, or only seem to win himself.[13]

This is existential freedom, not freedom to choose this or that but to choose oneself. We are so accustomed to thinking of choice in terms of selecting other people for something or choosing things to use or enjoy that it sounds nonsensical to speak of choosing oneself. Can anyone avoid being himself, except by committing suicide? Yes, in two ways. First, anyone can choose a style of life, make a personality for himself, that radically distinguishes the man of tomorrow from the man of yesterday. Second, anyone can refuse to consider a style of life that is already approved by others because they like it or because it is convenient, and can insist upon a life that he has worked out by himself and that he can justify on the basis of his own reasons. A man's existence is always his, of course, but the shape of his life can also be copied from others, so that his ideas and behavior are indistinguishable from theirs. He can refuse to go out on his own, and by refusing he will forfeit the life of inwardness that belongs to a human being. In this sense, Sartre overstates his case against the nature of man. An individual can choose his own character and way of life, but he cannot choose the necessity to choose; that is imposed on him as a human being and that is his human nature.

The existentialist, no matter how analytical in manner, is always issuing an urgent appeal to others to remember that each man's existence is his only, and that only he can make it what it is to be. When we look back at others, sum up their dispositions, efforts, and achievements, we judge them by what they decided to be. This accounts for the importance accorded passion by Kierkegaard and Feuerbach: "passion is the hallmark of existence."[14] "All existential problems are passionate problems"[15] — because the fullness of an awakened consciousness realizes that it is torn between finite and infinite interests, between what Tillich called preliminary and ultimate concerns. When Kierkegaard speaks of inwardness, it is not just as a synonym for what he called subjectivity; it was his special term for the subject's awareness of the tension between two radically different kinds of choice, one for this or that and the other for itself, its "infinite personal interest in an eternal happiness"[16] which, to Kierkegaard and Tillich, only God could satisfy.

The passionate man is not, therefore, a passively intense man but a man whose existence is defined by his choosing, his striving, his taking risks. No wonder Kierkegaard thought that existing was an art, and Jaspers, having read him carefully, borrowed his image of the leap to describe the radical breakthrough of a man from one kind of life to another. Jaspers borrowed another category as well, that of discontent, what used to be known as divine discontent, a discontent with finite or preliminary options and solutions. Tension between world and self experienced in existential inwardness — a special and complex form of introspection — is felt as dissatisfaction. What Augustine and Pascal called disquietude, Heidegger called care, that phenomenon the analysis of which is central to his thought, and which he took to be the very definition of human existence.

It is relatively easy to define existence in comparison with essence, human nature, or even the static notion of existence that is involved in saying that something is or is not. But this is still a definition from the outside. The insider's view of existence is something else again, and here is where we begin to take seriously Kierkegaard's assertion that existential reality is incommunicable and Heidegger's assertion that the self is both closest to us and farthest away. What is more, when we search literature and philosophy for descriptions of the sense of self, that raw, pure feeling for what it is to exist, instead of finding innumerable and memorable passages we find almost nothing. How could something that must be common to all men go so unremarked? Or is this intuition of self not common at all?

FLASHES

I can only answer — and present this — from my own experience. When I was a child I had the first of a series of brief, involuntary visions of my self as singular and mortal. So far as I can remember they were not products of any particular context, like an illness or other personal crisis. Suddenly my attention would be seized, insistently, intensely, totally, but too briefly for steady consideration. I

saw and understood, then was left shaken and relieved.
And yet I always remembered the moment clearly enough
to be able to reflect on its meaning. Each time it was the
same: I was given to understand that it was astonishing
that I existed at all on this earth, in this skin, at this time.
It seemed intolerable and scarcely credible that I, body and
mind, should be getting closer and closer to the time when
there would be no more I looking out into the world of sun
and streets. How would the world get along without me,
my center of consciousness, my caring? Each time I tried,
as I do even now, to remember what I felt so egocentrical-
ly, I became dissatisfied with my effort to recapture myself.
How could I express what I felt, the isolation, the watchfulness, the waiting, the certainty? I wondered whether
other people felt the way I did, and I supposed they might.
And yet, as I grew older, and particularly when I talked
about existentialism to students, I found that only a few
knew from their own experience what I was talking about.
What I took for granted meant nothing to most people I
met. I guessed that, lacking a foundation of self-
knowledge, they should not be expected to feel the urgency of existential questions, as Augustine, Pascal, and
Kierkegaard had.

That sharply defined look at myself as here rather than
in some other body and in some other part of the world,
at this time in history and not before or later, with these
feelings and these advantages, gave me the courage
to face the certainty of death squarely enough to insist that
my life not be frittered away on trivia. In spite of Dostoevsky's claim that one forgets this resolution in a day or so,
I did not. My resolution never lost either discontent or
passion. What is more, I understood when I was quite
young what lay beneath the passion of a lover or the ruth-
lessness of an artist. Nothing must be allowed to get in

the way of this chance to be and become oneself, least of all the safe rules and abstractions of those who have never learned that the first aspect of existence *(Existenz)* is that it is *mine*.

If there is self-centeredness in this, a suggestion of indifference, cruelty, or barrenness, let me say that the intuition of self was a unitary phenomenon of such magnitude and fullness from the start that I believed — and if I have ever had a faith it has been this — that it demanded a love of reality beyond myself, what Unamuno called a hunger of being, and that this hunger could only be fulfilled adequately through other persons. To be a person is to be in search of a person? No, it is to find a person and to be completely accepted, willingly and with benevolence, as God is said to accept man. I could understand why men prayed, why men went on spiritual quests, why they were in love with love, why rejection and silence were so destructive of the vitality and hopefulness springing from that basic intuition of self.

All this was confirmed for me — I knew I had a right to it — when at nineteen I first read Unamuno's *Tragic Sense of Life* and felt, as I still do, that even overblown hyperbole and illogical conclusions should not prevent recognition of "the thirst of being." If I was not as obsessed as Unamuno with immortality, a notion which has always seemed incredible to me, I was equally obsessed with the fantastic fact that I existed at all. I could not, as it seemed to me most people did, take it for granted and pass on to other things. For me it was not a resting place but a sure starting point for certain insights and convictions: in particular, the possibility of wasting one's life in view of the certainty of death, the resolution not to do so, but to seek passionately with mind, body, and heart for the tasks, the persons, the places that would be best for me.

Not even in Unamuno's writings could I find a description of this intuition of self. In two out-of-the-way places it cropped up, in Richard Hughes's *High Wind in Jamaica* and in the Notebooks of Gerard Manley Hopkins. From the former, "What agency had so ordered it that out of all the people in the world who she might have been, she was this particular one, this Emily: born in such and such a year out of all the years in Time, and encased in this particular rather pleasing little casket of flesh?"[17] And from the latter, "I find myself both as man and as myself something most determined and distinctive, at pitch, more distinctive and higher pitched than anything else I see; I find myself with my pleasures and pains, my powers and my experiences, my deserts and guilt, my shame and sense of beauty, my dangers, hopes, fears, and all my fate, more important to myself than anything I see. And when I ask where does all this throng and stack of being, so rich, so distinctive, so important, come from, nothing I see can answer me."[18] But in neither passage, nor in any other that I have read, is there mentioned the origin, in intuitive form, of my own resolution, under sentence of death, to concentrate on that kind of importance (unless Tolstoy's description of Ivan Ilych's death is a description of the way Tolstoy himself felt about life).

What Unamuno called "hunger of being" or "thirst of being"[19] I called nostalgia, a longing for what I had not yet experienced but could imagine, a homesickness not for the paradise that is lost but the paradise that might be. I later came across in Camus' notebooks the remark, which goes beyond the definition in *The Myth of Sisyphus*, that "nostalgia is the mark of the human,"[20] that "existence applies to something which is our nostalgia. . . . inexistential philosophy will be the philosophy of exile."[21] This term, initially confusing to those who associate nostalgia only with a harking back to the past and do not feel it as a pointing toward the future, not only sums up and sustains the resolution that is the moral consequence of the basic intuition of self, it carries with it an implicit answer to one of the most important questions that a man can ask of himself, "Can we get the whole of our being in our hands?" We can, and nostalgia is one phenomenon of the interior life that does this. It is not as universally experienced as the phenomenon Heidegger calls care (*Sorge*), but it is an outcropping of that, and far more intense, directed, and powerful. It takes over a person in such a way that his sense of existence does not remain underground but constantly compels him to seek and to select, meet and try.

MOMENTS

There are intuitions of the self, flashes of individuation less frequent but more memorable, that depend, very likely, on chemical imbalances. Both Dostoevsky and Nietzsche have left records of these. They are confirmed by the drug-induced states of countless young people today. It is a story of self-enlightenment, and so far as we are concerned here, the method hardly matters, whether it be contemplative self-discipline, drugs, or a disease like Dostoevsky's epilepsy. It is the content that matters, and there is some point to unfolding the story in a logical sequence.

Essentially it is a story of moments, flashes of wisdom and self-knowledge, rare and turbulent in process and effect. From an observer's point of view, that of Sartre, for example, it is possible to imagine the contrast between the humdrum and boring on the one hand and a life of the unexpected and adventure on the other — what Sartre called "privileged situations"[22] out of which "perfect moments"[23] can be seized. "At last an adventure happens to me and when I question myself I see that it happens that I am myself and that I am here; I am the one who splits the night, I am as happy as the hero of a novel."[24] But for Sartre the moment never arrives. His vision, as we shall see later, is essentially a negative one. The concept represents an ideal, and there are others for whom it is a reality.

Nietzsche knew this as both inspiration and ecstasy, although one must recognize that he could not sustain his personal ecstasy without converting it into a doctrine, a logical, and for him a redemptive conclusion, the eternal recurrence: "Inspiration, revelation, something profoundly convulsive and disturbing suddenly visible and audible with indescribable definiteness and exactness. One hears — one does not seek; one takes — one does not ask who gives: a thought flashes out like lightning. . . . There is an ecstasy whose terrific tension is sometimes released by a flood of tears. . . . There is the feeling that one is utterly out of hand. . . . There is a profound happiness in which the most painful and gloomy feelings are not discordant in effect. . . . This is my experience of inspiration. I have no doubt that I should have to go back millenniums to find another who could say to me: It is mine also!"[25] Of course the claim is extravagant. Nietzsche was neither the first nor the last to know ecstasy. It is interesting that in an earlier book he had written: "A kind of honesty has been alien to all founders of religions and others like them: they have never made their experiences a matter of conscience for knowledge. What did I really experience? What happened in me then, and around me? . . . We, however, we others who thirst for reason, want to look our experiences as straight in the eye as if they represented a scientific experiment. . . . We ourselves want to be our experiments and guinea pigs."[26] Unfortunately, Nietzsche was usually too impressed by his uniqueness to tell us more about the content of inspiration, beyond the depressing conviction — or was it really an intuition? — that "this life as you now live it and have lived it, you will have to live once more and innumerable times more; and there will be nothing new in it, but every pain and every joy and every thought and sigh and everything immeasurably small or great in your life must return to you — all in the same succession and sequence — even this spider and this moonlight between the trees, and even this moment and I myself."[27]

Not even that most individuated of men (to use a term Nietzsche used) ever described in any detail the content of the knowledge gained in one of those ecstatic moments of inspiration. It hardly needed special intuition to analyze with such destructive force the genealogy of morals and metaphysics; it needed a special brand of honesty and relentlessness with which Nietzsche was blessed. One must go back in time a little to Dostoevsky, to a confessedly diseased mind, to find a record of what the mind — and not only an epileptic mind — can see of itself and reality in general.

"There are moments — you can reach moments — when time suddenly stops and becomes eternal."[28] Dostoevsky did not mean what Nietzsche said he believed, that each moment recurs, but simply that time stops and everything can be comprehended for what it is. His was a vision of the present, not of all time, an experience of the unique opportunity each man has to exist, and, far more important, of man's capacity for cognitively embracing himself and Being. We might now call it a belief in the achievement of the Heideggerian quest for Being through self. In any case, Dostoevsky knew it at first hand, as we can see from his description in *The Idiot:* "His mind and heart were flooded by a dazzling light. . . . All his agitation, all his doubts and worries, seemed composed in a twinkling, culminating in a great calm, full of serene and harmonious joy and hope, full of understanding and the knowledge of the final cause."[29] "These moments, these flashes of intuition, those gleams and flashes of awareness" brought about "the highest mode of existence," "harmony and beauty," "completeness, proportion, reconciliation, and an ecstatic and prayerful fusion in the highest synthesis of life." "Those moments were merely an intense heightening of awareness, and at the same time of the most direct sensation of one's own existence to the most intense degree. . . . Yes, I could give my whole life for this moment."[30]

But of course, as he admitted, he did not and could not give his whole life for such moments; he recognized not only that they were byproducts of his disease but that everything unreconciled in life remained the same, to be dealt with in agony and frustration. It seems that in spite of the indubitable witness to the possibility of pure self-knowledge that Dostoevsky and others have made, the philosophical content is thinner than that of our own more pedestrian reflections. Intensity alone does not yield specific understanding. Sartre was right to be sceptical of "perfect moments." What good is a perfect moment if it leaves no traces, if one knows little more afterward than before? There is always some snare and delusion in mystical states and in peaks of self-enlightenment. Unless one can spell out the elements and parts of a vision, all one is left with is a recollection of intensity, however individuated, however grandiose. At the worst, as with Nietzsche and our drug culture, we can see genuine insight into self drowned in self-congratulation and smugness.

MYSTERY

The fact and fate of each man is too serious to be clouded over by indiscriminate ecstasies. It is far safer to begin more tentatively, as does Ionesco: "I have never quite succeeded in getting used to existence, whether it be the existence of the world or of other people, or above all myself."[31] This is the true mystery of the sense of self which is present in the inflation of ecstasy as well as the momentary flash of individuation of a child or an adult. It is modest and yet indicative of the impenetrability of the truly astonishing event that each of us is to himself. I have not read a more moving description of this than Ionesco's:

Sometimes it seems to me that the forms of life are suddenly emptied of their contents, reality is unreal, words are nothing
but sounds bereft of sense, these houses and this sky are no longer
anything but facades concealing nothing, people appear to be
moving about automatically and without reason; everything
seems to melt into thin air, everything is threatened — myself
included — by a silent and imminent collapse into I know not
what abyss, where there is no more night or day. What magic
power still holds it all together? And what does it all mean, this
appearance of movement, this appearance of light, these sorts of
objects, this sort of world? And yet there I am, surrounded by the
halo of creation, unable to embrace these insubstantial shades,
lost to understanding, out of my element, cut off from something undefinable without which everything spells deprivation.
I examine myself and see myself invaded by inconceivable
distress, by nameless regrets and inexplicable remorse, by a kind
of love, by a kind of hate, by a semblance of joy, by a strange
pity (for what? for whom?); I see myself torn apart by blind
forces rising from my innermost self and clashing in some
desperate unresolved conflict; and it seems I can identify myself with one or other of these, although I know quite well I am
not entirely this one or that (what do they want from me?), for
it is clear I can never know who I am, or why I am.[32]

This reflection on evanescence, companion to an equally threatening sense of solidity and presence (presence as solidity rather than responsiveness), is a necessary correction to the airy ebullience of the ecstatic moment. It brings one back to the actual isolated position of each person, whose isolation is so irredeemable that he instinctively finds ways to protect himself from facing it, the ways of ecstasy being but one of these ways. What Ionesco was writing about was contingency and a realization of the accidents of existence, impersonal and yet part of the definition of being a person. In this kind of reflection on existence he stands between the electrifying transparency of the mystic vision of reality that is Dostoevsky's — and perhaps Nietzsche's — and the dehumanizing nausea of Sartre. There is a wide gap between the man who cannot get used to existence and the man who says "existence is what I am afraid of."[33]

Indeed, there is a difference between being afraid of existence, either in the sense of being timid or living on the edge of suicide, and being put off, stuffed, suffocated with the impersonal contingency of reality, which does not distinguish between the kind of existence the self is and the kind the self lives with. Sartre's contingency is almost completely physical; it is his body, by which he is identified to himself, that looms so large that it almost blots out any other sense of self. I say almost, for when Roquentin says "I hadn't the right to exist. I had appeared by chance,"[34] there is at least the presumption that the "I" is more inclusive than the body and limbs that the "I" and eyes contemplate.

Nausea can arise out of concentration on matter, a hand, or a face, the root of a chestnut tree. If one stares long and fixedly enough, it is quite easy to find one's sense of the totality of form and matter split up, and the opaqueness of matter predominant. When one does this to oneself, the result is "nature without humanity," "nude existence," "obscene nakedness." Roquentin's logic is true to its method when he concludes, "I am the Thing."[35]

So this is what Sartre means by contingency. And yet much of the time he speaks of it as a metaphysician might. "I hadn't the right to exist. I had appeared by change." Whether such a statement represents detachment or whether it reflects some anguished intuition of birth and death, it still does not by itself lead to the obsession with formless matter that suffocates and nauseates Roquentin. Is the "fundamental absurdity"[36] that Sartre mentions the happen-so-ness of existence or is the detachment of matter from form, so that there is no definition, just a blob, a trick the mind plays on itself?

INSIGHT

It is impossible to say whether some kind of intuition of self — or of one's existence, if that seems different — always precedes the commitment to existential thought, whether in a philosopher or in a poet. But sooner or later one must retrace one's steps, in an order of increasing simplicity, until an understanding of the primary importance and complexity of this insight is reached. It may come in the night or in the day, to a child or to a grownup, once only or often. It may be the product of crisis or of gradually developing maturity; it may strike like lightning and strike blind; it may glow with all the warmth and fullness of a comprehension that would seem to make everything else pale and yet a part of it. It may be homely and individuated; it may be ecstatic and sublime. Whatever the manner, however long the duration, no matter how simple or how diverse the content, a sense of self, remembered or expressed, implicit or hidden and never to be revealed, is at the root of all existential thinking and passion.

There are moments, as Dostoevsky said, when something makes sense that explains everything else. From the outside — and we may think of ourselves from the outside — we are individuals and are contingent, here today, gone next week, with bodies and families and a world provided as if at random. As soon as a person, no matter how young, realizes that he is going to have to die, and that what he will be depends entirely on what he makes of himself and his opportunities, his real motive for passion and self-discipline is discovered. He will never be satisfied with anything less than the self that he will shape; and his dissatisfaction with anything less than that ideal, built on what he has been so mysteriously given, will motivate his seeking, his breathless wandering through his own wastes and the confusions of the world, in order to find his time, his place, and his identity.

Sartre : man is his own project —

the
major themes

2 INSECURITY

INSECURITY

When a series of writers in the nineteenth century became philosophically concerned about the insecurity of human existence, existentialism became a historical movement. From then on it has been normal to discuss the human condition in the terms which Pascal had introduced two centuries before, subjective and psychological. Metaphysical contingency has been reduced to a human scale as insecurity, and insecurity is understood as a state of mind and as a fact of existence. If there is one premise that binds existentialist thinkers together above all the rest, it is that there is a note of disquietude reverberating in the undercroft of consciousness.

What do Augustine, Pascal, Kierkegaard, Heidegger, Jaspers, Proust, Kafka, and Tillich have in common with each other (as well as with many poets, novelists, and theologians)? What but a preoccupation with radical interior insecurity? For Augustine it is restlessness, for Pascal feeling lost, for Kierkegaard melancholy and despair, for Heidegger care, for Jaspers boundary situations, for Tillich existential anxieties, for Kafka mistrust of self, for Proust anguish. These are but random samplings. Is life tragic? Is to live to suffer? The first question arises out of the second, and the second arises from a sense that even when no booby traps have been stepped on recently life still is inconclusive.

Beneath each moment of certainty there is a current that can drown out anything affirmative. Insecurity is the condition of human finitude. This is what Tillich meant when he said that it is estrangement rather than reconciliation that is the basic fact of human existence. We try to move towards the latter, but we start from and never permanently leave the former. Most people probably recognize this, whether they will say so or not. It is natural to suppress unpleasant insistent notes, even though it might be prudent in the long run to accept the *cantus firmus* and try to understand its meaning.

Each man should begin with his own feelings, although he is likely to learn more by comparing himself to a developed tradition. In the course of a lifetime of self-observation and reflection it would not be exceptional to experience most symptoms of insecurity that the literature of the philosophical imagination has given us. Any beginning is probably arbitrary. We can start with some of the simpler tensions of daily life — at least we like to think they are simple — the conflicts with others which are more or less inevitable, the frustrations of ambition, sexual tension, pressures from an accelerated and crowded urban life. Or we can begin with some form of guilt, self-mistrust, rejection accepted, taboos broken and confessed to, repeated failure. We can begin with more general threats to our identity as individuals — dangers from ill health and old age, war or job insecurity, or the more elusive problem of what or whom we can give ourselves to wholeheartedly, what can make us feel both free and fulfilled. There are innumerable starting points, and if the inner life of man is truly kaleidoscopic, it may make little difference in the end where one starts, provided that sooner or later the entire gamut of symptoms is run through and somehow connected.

The question is, of course, how one makes these connections. Is there an ontological or psychological order, a cosmic arrangement that will enable someone not accustomed to keeping balls juggling in the air to see *insecuritas* as a potentially complete, because inclusive, definition of human existence? This may be the wrong question. For even if there is no fate, no development in time, no structure of the self, there are a few ordinary distinctions that can be made. First, there is the difference between what is variously called ontological insecurity or metaphysical uneasiness and what should be called situational anxiety. There is also a difference between situations which are common to the human condition and special situations in which we all find ourselves from time to time. To illustrate the latter first, everyone must die, but not everyone is rejected by others or has difficulty knowing who he is. And yet the second kind of situation, not experienced by everyone, may be the occasion for the self to question itself as radically as it does in the first, inescapable, situation. In the end, what counts is not how the question is raised but how ultimate is the question that is raised. Anything that by chance makes a person feel isolated raises just as profound questions as does the prospect of death itself.

43 § insecurity

In the course of a man's life, there is no telling which kind of disquietude will surface first, ontological or situational. In the order of questionability, there is no doubt that ontological insecurity comes first, just because it is even more concerned with ultimates than is the certainty of death. For while there is nothing more final than death, the question of whether there is any end greater than oneself is more final — and even death becomes penultimate.

It would be misleading to suggest that only some kinds of insecurity and disquietude can yield ultimate questions. It would be wrong to criticize these distinctions by arguing that they are distinctions only by virtue of arbitrary definition of terms. These days even psychiatrists may speak of ontological insecurity or transcendence. We all have moments of uneasiness that, however poorly defined they are at the time and however specific their causes, trouble us because they remind us of a discontent that we cannot conceive of anything curing. For one who feels this way, whether he has any religious faith or not, the alternatives are philosophically clear: no ultimate satisfaction without some experience not yet conceivable, or a world in which the unexpected may yet happen.

RESTLESSNESS

St. Augustine's *Confessions* cannot be understood except along this line. Not only did he know many kinds of anxiety, but he had tried most of the well-known means of satisfaction. He had experience of sex, love, friendship, filial devotion, fatherhood, intellectual activity, travel, good food and wine, conversation, ecstatic visions, professional success. Nothing satisfied him for long. What is more, he always felt out of touch with his deepest self, unable to regulate his compulsive desires, particularly sexual ones, that clashed with his determination to find himself in some place of emotional tranquility. He was pragmatic enough to try everything. He knew everything his culture could offer, even himself, but without ever feeling that his knowledge or self-knowledge was ultimate. Something always seemed to elude both knowledge and self-control, and no amount of reading in philosophy or mysticism could satisfy him. His insecurity was what we call metaphysical, and could be relieved only through a total commitment to some way of life that transcended both action and knowledge. He had to lose himself before he could find himself, and that process, however we define it today, was a transcendental or religious one. The metaphysical unease was banished by religious conversion. His heart really was restless until it rested with God, which, in fact, meant until he threw himself on the ground in a friend's back yard and wept. He had found everything else he wanted, and remained as uneasy and miserable as ever. But he had not, until that day, found, because he had not looked for, humility. Worn out from looking elsewhere, he was so reduced and humiliated that he found a peace which proved to be lasting.

Augustine's case is an interesting one to us for several reasons. There has never been a man by nature more self-conscious and more gifted in self-analysis. He was an original, a pioneer. His pages on time and memory, on the divided moral self, on the elusive depths of the self were almost unprecedented. His insight into disquietude was so profound, so pervasive of every moment of consciousness, that it suggests that there really may be nothing we can do or think, no one whom we can meet, no social and political conditions so favorable, that we can remain free and at the same time find peace without tension and questionability — unless we take part in some experience that transcends seeking and finding. The only sort of experience that fits that definition is what theologians call grace, the gift of presence that sweeps an individual off his self-determined course. Nothing else could do that for Augustine, not his beloved mother, not his successful quest for wisdom, nothing but a turning by God, at least as he defined the happening which we call conversion. Mysterious, without a doubt, but so concrete that it would be unwise, for psychological reasons alone, to push it aside as irrelevant.

One last thing about Augustine — his disquietude was itself a strong thing, too strong to be called uneasiness, however metaphysical: "our hearts are restless until they can find peace in you"; "give me a lover, and he will understand"; "I was in love with love."[1] Twisting, tortured, trying this, trying that, demanding more of himself than of others, miserable with the results, the more successful and worldly wise he became. A man of intense, consuming passions — to compare oneself to this man is to risk looking ridiculous. And yet not to try would be to lose a chance to see the possibility of the depths of human helplessness, so profound that only religious terms are adequate to locate the place in experience where salvation occurs. Perhaps the experience would be more believable if we spoke more precisely of place and what happened there, the way to it and the way out, rather than repeating biblical words. The day may come when we will once again become familiar with the places where salvation occurs and finally abandon the anthropomorphic and abstract terms that speak of cause rather than process. When we do, then Augustine's testimony will perhaps at last come into the lives of the pragmatic as well as the pious.

CARE

It is one thing to reflect back over life, as Augustine did, and define existence in terms of what the course of life reduces one to; it is quite another to be able to look at a man's consciousness at any moment and define his being. This is what Heidegger has done, in his analysis of the phenomenon of consciousness he calls care. He took what he considered to be the most fundamental structure of the mind and separated its inseparable moments. To be conscious is to care. This means that each of us at all times cares about himself: a) about the fact that he has been thrown into the world, b) that he is in the world with others, and c) that he is always looking ahead. We cannot avoid feeling the contingency of existence, its impersonality. We have not given birth to ourselves; we are but parts of a remote, external momentum of nature and history. We did not provide our world either, but it is here, and we must accommodate ourselves to it. We cannot avoid a future, for we are always ahead of where we were when we started, and the only real question is what we are to do, where we are to go, what kind of being we are to become.

To care is also to feel tense — the tension first of all, of the three temporal aspects of care — for there is always conflict between the certainty that one is alive with others and must make choices involving them, and the uncertainty of a future coming out of a definite and unasked-for past.

There is also conflict between the uncertainty of the relationship to the world and self and the certainty of a death that will end all uncertainty. Having been put into the world, we can escape further tension only by running away from choices, and this obscures both the uncertainty of what to make of oneself and the certainty of one's death.

This temptation to seek some escape that will prevent one from being responsible for oneself, one's tensions, and one's destiny is what Heidegger calls the fall of man.

For Heidegger an authentic man is one whose sense of self — his conscience — calls him to do his own thinking and choosing, not to imitate, follow, and forget. This involves accepting death, recognizing that death is above all one's own, not related to anyone else, and not to be transcended. The man who accepts death as the final proof of his individuation is not only a being who can accept death, he is liberated for life, for, as Heidegger insists, death is not only a phenomenon of life, it reflects the very structure of man's existence, the structure of care. We are sent on death's way as soon as we are born, whether we like it or not. To live is to be about to die.

But this is insufficient without redefinition. To die is to live out the life of care, and care is where one is at all times until death. As a symptom of life's structures care is a mood of tension, uneasiness, conflict, uncertainty. It comprehends all three phases of time, the past from which we have come, the present with which we live, and the future which is always ahead. Thus it is impossible to speak of man's being, defined phenomenologically or psychologically, as care or disquietude, without thinking of time. There is nothing timeless about man; on the contrary, he is time-riven. Only in presence can time be forgotten and eternity imagined. But that is another story.

BOUNDARY SITUATIONS

The symbol of life as a search is a useful one, but its use may be quite different in the lives or thought of different men. Augustine, when he looked back on his life, saw it as a wandering and a seeking, tortuous, but relentlessly drawn and driven to a place and state of being where he could function freely and happily. The result was that he learned how to hold his whole being in his hands. Heidegger, on the other hand, set out to find out whether it is possible to talk sensibly about Being; the only clear result of his lifetime of reflection is that he showed others how to gather their whole consciousness, if not their whole Being, into their hands. His experience was comprehensive only in the manner in which it indicated a structure of our awareness of ourselves and our intentionality, as we idle along time's stream. It leaves out much that we all know, particularly the experiences which come under the heading of situational anxiety. Not only would we never know from reading Heidegger what it is like to live in the twentieth century — except by implication — we would also not know that Augustine's search for ontological security is still open to us, or that intimacy between people has ever been experienced, to say nothing of being desirable. Perhaps failure, self-rejection, even the differing responses to accusation, are implied in Heidegger's concepts of authenticity and conscience as a "call of care."[2] We would not have to guess about this if Heidegger's notion of experience did not leave relatively obscure that whole aspect of care which is our experience with others, for good or ill. Even phenomenology should be able to do better than this, should record the intake of consciousness as well as the abstract output called intentionality. If phenomenology is an inadequate method — and I think it is — it is because its users are men of impoverished or constrained social and interpersonal experience. It is not unusual to adopt a method that suits one's bias or one's fear of being unconventional.

There is, therefore, safety, if not excitement, in the unsystematic way Jaspers writes about existence, by way of typical situations in life that make it seem totally question-

able. His "boundary situations"[3] are not modes of consciousness but areas of living with ourselves and the world.
Where Heidegger is definitive, schematic, but abstract,
Jaspers is almost arbitrarily selective, but always concrete.
Beside Heidegger's densely structured analyses, Jaspers'
diffuseness makes him look like a dilettante. He tells us
what we already know, that we are always in one situation
or another, physical and psychological, and that we struggle, feel guilty, suffer, and die. He makes no effort to be
inclusive. Are these typical boundary situations? Are there
others? Many others? He does not say. He leaves us to ask
and to answer. What interests him is the effect these situations have on us.

When he tells us of the effects, he does not try to avoid
metaphors. He says that the ground is pulled from under
our feet, that we feel nothing is perfect, that we question
whether there is anything absolute and feel everything in
existence is open to question, that we can rest nowhere,
and that existence is inherently dubious and brittle. To
speak of a situation as a boundary situation is to remind
us that we can come to a line beyond which we are not permitted to pass, that foreign country lies there. And yet for
a time, at any rate, we cannot go backward either. We are
on the border. We can only become ourselves by standing
there with open eyes, and by regarding our existence
(*Existenz*), that which we and we alone can become.

Like Heidegger Jaspers advocates authenticity, and like
Heidegger (and Ionesco) he speaks of the discontent that
torments. He speaks of tension between self and world. He
writes, as Kierkegaard did, of a leap forward, of wrenching
oneself away with passion from anything that threatens to
make one a robot. There are great stakes in an existence
where I have to die, struggle, feel guilt, suffer, choose. Perhaps in the end these marks of passion bring him closer

to Kierkegaard and Augustine than to Heidegger, and his
insistence on our essential solitude in such situations en-
courages us to make use of tension, rather than accommodate ourselves to it by pretending it is not always with
us.

ANXIETIES

Tillich not only breaks down Jaspers' situations into three
types of existential anxiety, he approaches the existence of
man like Heidegger from the perspective of consciousness,
instead of from the perspective of situations that impinge
on consciousness. At the same time he focuses on man as
he becomes aware of threats to his authenticity, in the three
areas of morality, meaning, and factual existence. Accordingly, Tillich defines man in terms of threats to being
rather than opportunities for being. In the end, his injunc-
tions to accept the unacceptable, death, guilt, meaninglessness, is an affirmation of life and self. We are torn between
relative and absolute, partial and total threats, all unavoidable and yet, except for death, none unconquerable; we
are creatures of fate and chance, mismanagers of our lives
and society sometimes to the point of total self-disgust,
constantly discovering the emptiness of means and ends
and sometimes faced with the possibility that all effort and
all thought are in vain. We have the choice, both Heidegger
and Jaspers insisted, of facing up or running away. Tillich
understood neurotic anxiety as a way of preventing existential anxieties from coming to the surface where they
would have to be dealt with in their own terrible terms.
There are, of course, other techniques of evasion — Pascal's
paragraphs on diversion remind us of our own — that are
just as effective in holding reality at bay.

These three existential philosophers promise no security. They proceed, each in his own way, from an analysis of the self in crisis to some determination of one's being that separates one from the crowd. They are in spirit completely Kierkegaardian, as was Barth and his so-called crisis theology: "the whole concrete world is ambiguous and under crisis";[4] "the insecurity of our whole existence, the vanity and utter questionableness of all that is and of what we are, lie as in a textbook open before us."[5] For this Pauline man, this Kierkegaardian, the theme of theology itself is "men in their final distress and hope."[6] It is probably no accident that these four thinkers should have discovered Kierkegaard at the same time, during World War I, and that their analyses of human existence should be so strikingly similar. The shock to civilized man of that cataclysm seems to have had greater spiritual effects than any political event since the French Revolution. Existentialism was a product of that war.

So much in agreement were the philosophers and theologians of that generation that it has been difficult to reflect on human existence in their shadow without using their perspectives, and to look for a way to organize other experiences of insecurity which at times are more important to us. If all we know of interior experience came from reading Heidegger, we might feel under an impossible compulsion to be authentic, to choose oneself, in total disregard of any particular form of disquieted consciousness. Of course, it would still be possible to be aware of a three-fold intentionality, the given, the others, and the future, but the nature of both the given and the character of the others around us makes all the difference when we come to projecting ourselves from one moment to the next.

Similarly, it is convenient to think of inner suffering in the ordered terms of a three-fold threat to being: existential anxieties responding to existential situations, moral, spiritual, ontological. But it is the particular threat that has to be faced, accepted, or rejected, and one cannot do this abstractly. We must know the nature of a threat, the nature of each situation and its own anxiety. Both Jaspers and Tillich offer us only a schema of sorts, and we are left with the task of defining specific anxieties, which in some cases seem to belong to more than one of their types of situation. Where does one place the fear of job failure? Is it a moral anxiety, or does it open up the question of personal emptiness, a life without meaning, and a person without identity? Where, for that matter, do any of the concerns about identity, and its crises, fall? They clutch the nerves as if the very body were being attacked. And so it can be, if the sense of self shrinks to the point where life becomes paralyzed and the self cut off, as if by fate, from any help in self-recognition. Death is then not far off, and a living death, ontological zero, becomes more than a metaphor.

On the other hand, however much we ourselves are impressed and exhilarated by the formula and success of Augustine's religious disquietude, there is an ideological remoteness about it for many contemporary men and women. Leaving aside the question of the reality of God and prayer, our contemporaries are not easily convinced that disquietude can be understood in any terms other than emotional ones. Disquietude can be an acknowledged part of human life without suggesting, as it did for Augustine, the void of eternity.

INTERPRETATION

It is a truism to say, as Jaspers does, that we are always in some situation or other. It is more arguable that we are always bearing some form of disquietude or anxiety. Whether the ultimate point of insecurity, apart from warning us of danger, is to lead us to heaven by way of a new life on earth (or whether heaven is a new life on earth), the causality of disquietude and the course it can take are two problems worth reflecting over. Anxieties are the stuff of our lives, preventing peace, love, and justice, menacing peace, love, and justice, and with their pain making us dream of peace, love, and justice. Never totally absent, it is hardly imaginable that their causes can ever be erased or permanently controlled. The sophisticated man knows he is never finally safe, even though periods of reprieve obscure the worst for a while.

Clearly there is a distinction to be made between a faint and wavering unease of the spirit and a heavy, constant, demanding anguish or melancholy. There is also a difference between the ability of a person to keep on functioning, holding his anguish at arm's length, and a final surrender in depression or despair. This is a course over which the inner life runs which every mature person should be aware of, so that he can be warned by danger signals, so that, in fact, he may know whether a faint malaise is a symptom of deeper trouble or just of some relatively easily handled tension that does not touch the heart of his being.

Thus the young man in Kafka's *The Castle* who "thought nothing but the Castle day and night. . . . it turned out that it wasn't really the Castle he was thinking of, but the daughter of a charwoman in the offices up there."[7] How much metaphysical tension might turn out to be sexual need? For that matter, how much anxiety is simply the result of a chemical imbalance of some sort? Probably a great deal, as anyone can testify who has taken consciousness-changing drugs, whether because of illness or as an experiment.

Nevertheless, the question of causality is not to be put aside that easily. Even the satisfaction of sexual desire may still leave metaphysical need — or romantic need — whether the uneasiness is ever understood as metaphysical, whether uneasiness is admitted to at all. The question is whether there are conflicts that give rise to tensions, pressures that make for uneasiness, not whether it is possible to obliterate one tension temporarily by satisfying another. At the bottom of the scale of tension is the boredom of the man who waits, impatiently or indifferently, for something to happen, someone to turn up. Having decided that life must finally come to him, not he to life, he has so misconceived the requirements of his structure of care that he knows something has gone wrong. But what is wrong is not that something has not happened, but that he will not move out of his way station into a future, taking the initiative to make things happen. Fatigue or failure, of course, may excuse his attitude, but it is more likely that he has enjoyed the easy cost of justification by misery. And so he drifts, bored, miserable, uncertain of everything except that nothing worthwhile depends on himself.

Compare this aimless floating or standing around disgruntled with the more demoralized suspension of one who has reached a period in life when he is unsure of others, his relationship to them, the course of history, the viability of values he once took for granted, the whole order or disorder of the cosmos. In this list are different sources of anxiety, which one can respond to faintly or firmly, in disquietude or in anguish, partially or fully. Indeed, Pascal, who could have been the inspiration for such a list, was only too conscious of the different reasons for similar emotional registrations.

Pascalian man is just man, whose condition is "inconstancy, weariness, unrest."[8] If ever there was a man without illusion — one for Camus to respect — it was Pascal, and he never humiliated his reason (*pace* Camus), however he may have humbled his heart in prayer. In entry after entry of the *Pensées* we see the swirling emotional life of man, boredom, vanity, uncertainty, deception and self-deception, inconstancy, playthings of the cosmos or creatures lost in an impersonal cosmic wood too large to take in, too alien for intimacy. And for all that there is an idea of God, but only an idea, that reason cannot give flesh to. Fortunate the man, one might say cynically, who is not as sure of what is at stake as is Pascal, and is spared his metaphysical anxiety. Fortunate the man who is not alarmed by the eternal, empty spaces, who does not see himself and his surroundings drifting, spinning. Fortunate the man who would not know what we are talking about, for whom there is no uncertainty about absolutes because only the relative is real, who never feels metaphysically dizzy because he plods along on the firm ground of the expected, who never feels lost because he continually hears sounds that tell him he is where he ought to be. And how unlike the man who, before he is found, knows he is lost.

Pascal would have agreed. He too was lost, but he was able to make life viable and to give it some sense of destiny by putting himself into the hands of the Church, its life of prayer and sacraments, its way of humility and charity. The rest, the experience of the present, which he claimed man wants but does not have, he was also able to know — we cannot say achieve — in that same religious way and in his mystical moments. It is important not to be sidetracked by the diversity of the emotions of unease that affected Pascal and to miss the common note of metaphysical estrangement. No matter how polemical, he was not a man whose philosophical preoccupation with disquietude included the effects of fate and necessity or the acceptance of a moral judgment against the self. He came as near, centuries ahead of us, to illustrating Tillich's anxiety of meaninglessness as any man ever has. Even his harsh references to the death to which each man is condemned derive their persuasive power from the part they play in his dominant obsession with a life that must either have meaning or not have meaning. Death gives one little time to make up one's mind and choose a way of life that makes sense.

DEATH

Indeed, if we pass from Pascal's *Pensées* to Tolstoy's "The Death of Ivan Ilych" or Rilke's *Malte Laurids Brigge*, we find the atmosphere quite different. Death does black every other question out, and becomes the center of care. For Pascal, his feeling of being lost in the universe affects all else, including death. But he, like Camus, was more interested in meaning, in what makes life worth living. However impatient he might be with those who forgot their mortality, he never matched the graphic eloquence of Tolstoy and Rilke in their descriptions of "a death of one's own."[9] Most of us are far enough away from death not to have to think about it; it is only when it comes near that it makes every other concern seem trivial. The same cannot be said of moral and spiritual problems.

When one knows he is to have "a death of one's own," death becomes at the same time "It," the "Big Thing," "the only reality." When one knows one has to die — knows from inside so that there is no gap between knower and known — the new loneliness forces new questions about life. "When I am not, what will there be?" "How is one to understand it?" "What if my whole life had been wrong?"[10] The despair in the first two questions is deepened by the fear of failure in the third.

From this point of view it makes sense to say that the question of meaning is the most important question of all and that if anxiety leads us to ask it, it is worth having. The question of meaning can be raised too late, as with Ivan Ilych himself, who had led a conventional, unthinking life, and then it only had the result of reminding him of what might have been. The question of meaning does not, on its side, often enough have the force required to propel it as far as it should go because people are not really convinced of the short time they have to pursue a destiny in a world in which it is only too easy to be careless.

The most common form of disquietude, irritability, should also be taken seriously, as a sign of deep impatience with the shortness of time in which to work out our life plan. This is only an example of the care with which one must distinguish between occasional disquietude and constant melancholy, as if the first were less significant than the second. For irritability can disappear once a plan is being worked on, the task set and accomplished, and yet while it is present it can block the entrance of a dark cavern in a person's life, the need to fulfill himself.

This is what Kierkegaard meant by melancholy, his castle and his mistress. Melancholy is a theme that runs throughout his writings. It is not one phenomenon but several, but as he first wrote about it, before it became a symbol of his own self-isolation and self-torture, it stood for "a hysteria of the spirit,"[11] a stage in the development of the inner life where one no longer can drift along absorbing what the world offers but is ready to strike out for some measure and sense of destiny, one's eternal validity. In saying that there is something inexplicable about melancholy, in spite of the fact that people so often wallow in it,

Kierkegaard was tracing an invisible line between the self that is unawakened to its selfhood and the self which is being nudged awake. In this respect, melancholy is a premonition of the full-blown, passionate restlessness that compelled Augustine to seek God for ten years. Compared to this spirit, melancholy is weak and contemptible. No wonder that Kierkegaard, unwilling to abandon his self-isolation from God and men, came to think of his own melancholy, bordering constantly on despair, as a madness he was born with, so much a part of his personality that he could not imagine himself without it. He could see salvation in the abstract and cling to bitterness in the concrete. It was his vocation to say "no" for himself, while saying "yes" for others.

IDENTITY

So far we have been considering either situations or occasional, even momentary, reminders of the fundamental isolation and responsibility of selfhood. But in the course of everyday existence they are not as telling as the persistent sources of insecurity that are caused by other people's meanness or aggression. It is here that the existential philosophers have little to say, and one can learn more from Kafka and Proust than from Heidegger, Jaspers, Tillich, and even Kierkegaard. Moreover, apart from the constancy and frequency of this fear of others, questions of identity and life's meanings in an indirect way suggest the path of salvation, at a time when it is increasingly difficult to look to any form of immortality as an answer to the question of death or to any form of God as an answer to the question of meaning. As long as this is the case — and there is no particular reason to think that it will not be the case from now on — death can be faced openly and ultimate meaninglessness confessed without despair, but only if the third form of anxiety is understood and dealt with. And that will be difficult enough.

When one looks at the range of feelings that record questions about one's identity and dignity, one begins to suspect that Tillich may have misled us in offering an all-inclusive division of anxieties into these three. Whether there is a fourth, an offshoot of the moral dimension of man, is not as important a question as whether there is any place in this scheme to discuss the central issue of who we are. Tillich might have claimed that who we are, and whether we are recognized or not, depends on our worth, that our sense of self and dignity is intimately bound up with our use of freedom. But that is to overlook an underlying pre-occupation of all men with their identity, their distinctiveness among others, proved by a kaleidoscope of experience and testified to by the acclaim of one's fellows. Each of us wants to know who he is, to feel he is different and to know the difference, and to know that at least one other person sees this, even if he does not like what he sees. The ultimate insult is to be passed by.

A great part of Proust's series of novels is devoted to descriptions of the anguish induced by being snubbed or betrayed. Gabriel Marcel has said, "We live in a world where betrayal is possible at every moment."[12] As people grow older, experience teaches them to be afraid that others will forget them when they are not around. The busier we are, the easier it is to put out of mind even our closest friends. It takes little imagination to fear that, once dead, we too will be utterly forgotten. For most people there is a special terror embedded in this fear, the terror of losing a last chance to have an identity confirmed.

Proustian anguish is of two kinds, that arising from rejection and that related to the interior search for identity.

Proust knew that when the first fails one should be able to fall back on the second. But the second depends to some extent on the degree to which one has been able to obliterate the anguish of indifference, rejection, or betrayal. Age and time do heal in that sense, and so if the Proustian quest is successful, and one learns to value the moments of involuntary recall — the recapture of the past as if present — then one's identity, involving a whole world of memories, can be comprehended in a fiction of concentrated and yet complex vision. All is present, and interrelated, as one person, one event, one feeling, with the identity of the self not only assured but controlling the filming of its history. So the question which is implicit in Heidegger, how can I get my life into my hands, had been answered by Proust: by memory and fiction. Heidegger himself called it understanding the schema of care.

A schema does not satisfy the quest for identity; it merely outlines the nature of the problem, the problem of decision and projection, of creative effort. The Proustian quest, no matter how successful, does not satisfy the quest for identity because his sense of presence is memory rather than encounter. Rejection can be final, snubs can hurt so much that the nerves become exquisitely tender. Betrayal can destroy habits of trust and in the end prevent the flowering of the basic self-confidence that must accompany a sense of identity. I am not real if nobody thinks I am, for how can I then be sure that my self-confidence is more than wishful thinking?

This is the reason why the sickness of jealousy, which is at the bottom of lovesickness, is so crucial. The vertigo suffered by a person who is frightened because he feels lost in the immense spaces of the cosmos or in the reaches of history and its clashing ideas is not nearly as disabling as the dizziness experienced by a person who has lost what he considers is his main hope of being recognized as a person of some weight and fullness. Collapse is imminent, recovery very hard, for nothing makes one more vulnerable to permanent instability than the experience of being turned away. Meanings come and go, and one can be eternally hopeful that a better idea or ideal will come along. Guilt is incurred and forgiven. Sickness and death threaten, and recede, and are soon forgotten. But in the stillness of being ignored, there is nowhere to turn. "Do you know what it is to have nowhere to turn to?" asks Marmeladov in *Crime and Punishment*.[13]

REJECTION

The existential categories of our time are those of identity, recognition, homelessness, loneliness, failure, self-rejection, and depression. One way to indicate the validity of this list is to compare the Kierkegaardian or even Tillichian notion of despair with depression. Tillich may have a point when he says that it takes some courage to despair, but one would hardly say that courage has anything to do with depression, that combination of despair and inertia. The causes of the two are different. Despair is the echo of slamming of doors to a room from which there is no exit. One can still rage and fume inside the room when he knows the doors can be opened by someone else. It is quite different with depression. When the sense of identity is choked up, breathing itself is almost impossible.

Perhaps, in this sense at least, Heidegger's analysis of care is relevant. When we no longer feel the reality of the world into which we have been inserted, because it takes no notice of us, then it is impossible to move toward the future. There is no future when one is cut off from the world in which one must participate in order to survive as a person.

Lucky the betrayed man who can fight back, the jealous man who can still show anger, the homeless man who is still homesick. Perhaps lucky too the depressed man who can be kept on ice until someone else, in love or in therapy, can reach him and lead him gently back into the world. Worst off is he who has been convinced by others that he is no good, who believes what he has heard, and is not to be persuaded by overt gestures of approval or affection. He is truly a prisoner of rejection.

Kafka was such a one. Whatever his temperamental predispositions, his chemical imbalance, he was less able than most to endure a father's contempt. Fear of condemnation became compounded with the conviction that his father's judgment was correct, that he really was worthless. Self-mistrust, the belief that he was worth nothing, that he could be nothing but a failure, became so ingrained that neither his mother nor that extraordinarily understanding friend Milena Jesenska could free him from it.[14] The story of an emotional improvement during his last illness, his life with Dora Dymant, is incomplete and only contributes one more piece to the puzzle of his life.[15] Was it really Dora's love that produced the change, or was it the result of his tuberculosis?

Kafka's "fear,"[16] a mistrust of self so complete that he could think of himself in relation to Milena as an animal groveling in the forest — "love is to me that you are the knife that I turn within myself"[17] — is not a type of anxiety that middle America can read about with much sympathy. It sounds sick and unmanly. Yet middle America's concern with security and failure, identity and recognition, is a mighty symptom of a shaky condition that we all wish we could stabilize. One has only to know a few people really well to notice their desperate and only partially successful attempts to be assured of a viable identity, their longing to belong and to be welcome, to be treated as if they mattered to someone else, and underneath that extraordinary vulnerability to slight and its consequent isolation and loneliness. Tillich's abstract formula for forgiveness, "accepting the unacceptable,"[18] misses the real point about rejection. It takes two to release and heal. You cannot accept yourself if no one else is willing to do so with you. And in a time of no God, it is quite impossible to expect God to act on behalf of us whose proper business it is to restore what we ourselves removed, recognition and respect.

So again it must be said that depression is not the worst experience, even though it may be worse than despair. Self-rejection and the nightmares that are born out of the self's vulnerability are the worst. Kafka's books, his fictions of life, are rightly said to be nightmares of the spirit, under some kind of control that other men do not have. Perhaps this is how he retained enough health to be healed in the end. Perhaps, like Sartre's Roquentin, Joseph K., keeping his intelligence clear to the end, was preparing for another adventure, a new fiction that would restore reality. Perhaps Milena was herself too like her friend, too capable of understanding what she could not heal, the labyrinthine ways of his conscience.

Kafka did not die in a Nazi concentration camp as she did, nor were his nerves so shrilly assaulted by pressures and acceleration as ours. His witness and story are simpler, although perhaps no less cogent, than those of men living today, who may not even feel the intensity and concentration of a malignant indifference of Father or God, and who are left on their own to find themselves, in fear and trembling. It is hard to imagine a more radical setting for existential anxiety than our own.

If we take them "mimetically."

the
major themes

3 THE VOID

THE DEAD GOD

Whoever believes in God cannot know ultimate loneliness. Whoever has not yet faced a future emptied of those who care for him does not know ultimate loneliness either, and is hardly likely to sense the void left by the passing of God. Not all existentialists have responded openly to this aspect of our recent cultural past. We must do it for them. Their insights into the spectrum of darkness are not as profound as those of Kafka, who in his "fear" felt the full force not only of human rejection but of cosmic indifference as well. He was not merely fearful, he was, except in his writing, disabled. It can be said that this is not an age of anxiety but an age of emotional and spiritual disability. The difference is considerable.

Buber, Marcel, Tillich, Jaspers — compared to Kafka and Heidegger — seem not even to have felt the irony of Pascal's

?

skepticism, to say nothing of Nietzsche's nihilism. It is difficult to understand how anyone can mention God complacently after reading Pascal, how anyone can talk of God at all after reading Nietzsche. Does an experience of radical human loneliness have to precede the conclusion that there is no God, or is it possible to be immune to the spiritual climate of one's time? After all, Nietzsche had warned us that it would take time before the death of God would reach our ears.

Pascal, of course, did not believe God was dead. He knew he could not see or know him. God is, but is hidden. "If there is no God, He is infinitely incomprehensible. We are incapable of knowing either what He is or if He is."[1] We are almost equally incapable of knowing what we are. We live in darkness, and we are ourselves full of darkness. Lost in some corner of a silent universe, we can only imagine a God who himself is lost, and whom only the heart can reach, reason being powerless and misleading.

Many years had to go by before men wondered whether there was any difference between a hidden God and no God at all — whether, if reason could not know, the heart could, whether longing was not wishful thinking. But when the question was finally clearly asked by Nietzsche, the answer came back fast enough. What is extraordinary is not that it took so long to ask but that it has taken so long to understand the question. Nietzsche has been read for seventy years now, and many of his admirers — among whom one would have to place many theologians — still are not willing to say "of course, it should have occurred to me long ago," so rooted are minds in the ideas of the past, or perhaps, as Nietzsche himself said, "I'm afraid we are still not rid of God because we still have faith in grammar."[2]

At least Pascal — and Ingmar Bergman and Unamuno — understood their own ambivalence. As Lucien Goldmann has pointed out, for Pascal God was at all times both absent and present. This was the source of the conflict between his faith and his skepticism. Both were real, thus the Pascalian anguish. Bergman's Knight asks, "Why can't I kill God within me. . . . What is going to happen to those of us who want to believe but aren't able to?"[3] The idea of God takes a distressingly long time to die, and yet when death comes it can come swiftly. Unamuno's life seems to have been devoted to the impossible task of promoting a concept of God which his reason could accept even less than Pascal's, in order to suggest a guarantee for the immortality of his consciousness, an immortality which his reason could also not accept. Pascal, at least, did believe from the heart; Unamuno could not.

Whatever the difference, and it is considerable, their sense of the abyss was quite distinct from Dostoevsky's and Nietzsche's. In spite of the superficial orthodoxy of Dostoevsky, he, not Nietzsche, was the first to outline the consequences of the absence of God and immortality. He had no illusions: absence meant void and vacuum. An abyss between head and heart may be infinite, but it is totally unlike the spiritual emptiness that surrounds one who no longer believes in the reality of God. Such a person is not easily convinced that the existence of other men will reduce the burden of his loneliness. If others like ourselves are all we can know, then we are truly alone, unless we are capable of responding to them and they to us, as true "religious" respond to God.

That is the problem, and it is as much a problem for the future as it was for Dostoevsky and Nietzsche. Can one live in a vacuum, a place from which God has been sucked out, and not be at the mercy of every slight and snub, each making the inner man more nervous and more vulnerable than the last? Nietzsche thought not: "you will never pray again, never adore again, never again rest in endless trust; you have no perpetual guardian and friend for your seven solitudes."[4] We know that Buber, for one, had a different answer, but although we can respect his reply, he would be more convincing if we could feel that he knew the Nietzschean and Kafkan experiences from the inside. It is easy to introduce "the eternal Thou"[5] when one has been able to experience presence with other human beings. But what has made this experience possible in a time of no God, no eternal Thou? Is it enough to say that Nietzsche was only doing what had to be done, killing off a God who was a conceptual It so that the true, the real God who is with You can be felt? Perhaps. But if so, we are left with the mystery of the disabled, of Nietzsche himself, of Kafka, and all the rest of those who, as Proust said, cannot emerge from themselves to meet someone and live with his presence.

Perhaps there is no mystery at all. Perhaps we should expect a gap here between the time when the mind suddenly loses faith in the incredible and the time when it becomes accustomed to looking for its health elsewhere. Who can adjust to such a change, such a debasement of his idea of God, and such an exaltation of his idea of his experience with another? However this may be, the certainty of the void coexists with the isolation of modern man, and it is unwise to assume too quickly that the coincidence is accidental.

MORAL VACUUM

It was some years before Dostoevsky realized that there might be a connection between a spiritual void and a moral vacuum. The moral symptoms he knew early, as early as *Notes from Underground*, but he seems to have concluded only that moral schizophrenia was a consequence of living in the nineteenth century. What it was about that century that made it so different he did not know — that is, not until he came to write *The Possessed* and *The Brothers Karamazov*. Then it was clear to him that a man who no longer believes in God (and, he always added, immortality) might feel free, might even feel obliged, in order to prove his freedom, to be a sadist or a masochist. Although we can say, with some degree of truth, that sadism and masochism were consequences of psychological defects in Dostoevsky himself, nevertheless he is not unconvincing when he asks what barriers are left once you have taken absolutes away. He then turns the question around and suggests that it is difficult to live in the nineteenth century and believe in God, and that once God's absence is admitted, a man is free to do as he pleases.

The Dostoevskian characters whose pleasure it is to be kind to their neighbors are no more impressive to us than to Dostoevsky. Those who admit their love for evil, for Sodom, for parricide, seduction of minors — for, in short, the worst their traditional sense of beauty and goodness could imagine — are also the most energetic. But once liberated by the death of the idea of God, free only to do evil, they either kill themselves or go mad.

There is a historical process at work here. The French revolutionaries were as conscious of the death of God and traditional morality as were Dostoevsky and Nietzsche a century later. Liberation has many meanings, and the least one can do is assume, until proof to the contrary is really available, that, causality aside, there are simultaneous associations among economic, political, psychological, philosophical, and religious liberations. It is the historian's un-enviable task to try to unravel them. Philosophers should note that several centuries after radical skepticism first addressed itself to the question of the absolute of absolutes, it is still possible for educated men to act as though the question had never been raised. But then our part of the twentieth century might be characterized, for many people, by a "leave-of-absence" phenomenon, a waiting without hope, but without despair either.

THE ABSURD

In this respect Camus' notion of the absurd is timely, although not a complete parallel. For him man in our time — and he did not in theory exclude the possibility of the recovery of absolutes — was torn between the nostalgia of the heart for truth and justice and the unreasoning silence of a murderous world. He had no ultimate hope, and no illusions. He thought that the best living was the most living, and that revolt, passion, and intellectual lucidity alone could provide the vitality needed to keep the absurd tension from collapsing. If it were to collapse, then nostalgia would sink into despair or be humiliated by religious or metaphysical faith. He preferred the honesty of lucidity, a Kafkan honesty in the face of injustice and ambiguity.

But it must be pointed out that Camus' absurd is not the same as a vacuum. As he himself said, the rebel can say *no* because (in some way) he has already said *yes*. Camus is an affirmative thinker, he said *yes* to many things, to love as well as to justice, to the sand, sea, and sun, to many people, to the future of man. He was as fascinated by Kafka as Buber, for just as Buber could see the God of the concentration camps prefigured in the Law that Kafka hated and worshipped, so Camus could respond to what he thought was Kafka's nostalgia for a lost paradise even more than to his peculiar kind of resignation. How often we have found ourselves borrowing something from another mind and ignoring that mind's clear challenge to some illusion of our own.

In this sense even Kafka was not ready to listen to Nietzsche. The latter once quoted Epicurus, an apocryphal Epicurus, as saying "if there are gods they do not care for us." One might imagine Kafka saying "if there is God, he hates us." And yet it was Kafka who cared, not Nietzsche, who found the quotation amusing. Kafka's Law is real enough. He does not need to call it God; as the Law, it lives somewhere between God and human dignity; it challenges the latter, questions it, persuades it to seek conformation outside itself, and carefully avoids contact with it. This is a negative God, a God, that is, like a photographic negative, with all qualities in reverse except absoluteness, absolutely negative.

There is a distinction currently made between the experience of the absence of God and the absence of the experience of God. Camus and Sartre had no experience of God, and they could not be said to have experienced the absence of God. Bergman and Unamuno could. Kafka does not fit here at all. However radical his theology — putting aside the question of the appropriateness of using the word theology — his experience was not so much of absence as of concrete, living, active rejection. The Law was his symbol for the authority of his life that convinced him that his being rejected was both justified and obscene. The negative God was not absent for Kafka but was part of his whole life and estimate of himself. He could not envisage life without its senseless governance.

THE END OF METAPHYSICS

It might well be asked which is worse, a dead God or a negative God, life in the shadow of rejection or life at the edge of the void, some attention or no attention. The choice is not usually ours to make, any more than it was for Kafka and Nietzsche. The life of neither is enviable enough to use as a model. The difference may be a philosophical one in any case. Can one live in a time of no God, as the theologians put it, and live with God, absent or negative, hidden or malevolent? Or is it just sleight of hand, so to speak, when someone raises rejection and self-rejection to the level of divinity? As Kafka said of the young man that it was not the Castle but only the daughter of the charwoman, so we can say that there was no Law but only a tyrannical father Kafka took too seriously. Let us not be too critical; by Kafka's stripes some of us may yet be healed.

Kierkegaard has reminded us that we love to hear the sweet anguish of the poet; we ask him to sing and suffer so that he may sing the more sweetly, not only for our pleasure but for our salvation as well! Across death, men like Kafka and Nietzsche are our companions; for all practical purposes they are presences. Their drama is our psychodrama; we act out our own illnesses through plotting the graphs of their diseases. Better an understanding of someone else than no understanding of ourselves? Rather some understanding of ourselves through understanding them. And yet how remote they actually are to us, the times in which they lived, their families, their dispositions, their friends, their talents. They were, we must remind ourselves, true isolates. If we are tempted to admire them because they did not continually weep for themselves — if we are disappointed because on occasion they did weep for themselves — we would be presumptuous to demand of them, most of all of Nietzsche, the strength to endure an experience of the void so overwhelming that even now we feel safe in contemplating it only when we admire the completeness and clarity of their insights.

From his first book, *The Birth of Tragedy*, to the end, before illness paralysed his mind, one thing above all was clear to Nietzsche; there was only Becoming, no Being. What he at first called "the Dionysian substratum of the world,"[6] individuation, terror and horror, flux, are the nature of reality. Mankind has had only two choices, to recognize and accept this or to deceive itself in order to avoid terror. Nietzsche spent his life uncovering the deceptions of history, the desperate and, to him, shameful attempts to believe in an order of reality for which only faith is evidence.

His own development of destructive criticism passed from a euphoric period when he depended on metaphors to express his discovery of the unreality of God, Being, Another World, to his later systematic criticism of the psychological motives for religious and metaphysical belief and the probable cause of its disappearance. It was one thing to say "God is dead," and another to show what that meant. What ought to be felt as relief was in fact experienced as a radical nihilism that would leave mankind homeless for many years to come and would be followed by a reexamination of all values.

How lightly and how gaily he sketched, in *The Twilight of the Idols*, the stages of disillusionment about a "true world," once "attainable for the sage, the pious, the virtuous man; he lives in it, he is it," to the day when it is "an idea which is no longer good for anything, not even obligating — an idea which has become useless and superfluous."[7] But the sketch fails to bring to life the radical nihilism that opens up a psychological void for civilized men and women, accustomed to the consolation of what they thought were experiences of transcendence. For that matter, Nietzsche's rhetoric makes one wonder whether he fully understood, in his pride at being a pioneer, how desperately mankind had felt the need of something transcendent to cancel out the pain of individuation.

And yet when we read the notes in *The Will to Power* which outline the withdrawal of an assurance of meaning in all events, of a structure within events, of a permanence beyond empirical evidence, we can believe that he knew — regardless of what he may have felt — what he was talking about: "now one realizes that becoming aims at nothing and achieves nothing"; "at bottom man has lost the faith in his own value when no infinitely valuable whole works through him."[8] This is a far cry from his earlier conclusion that life is "not all sad and dark, but rather like a new, scarcely describable kind of light, happiness, relief, exhilaration, encouragement, dawn. Indeed, we philosophers and 'free spirits' feel as if a new dawn were shining on us when we receive the tidings that 'the old god is dead'; our heart overflows with gratitude, amazement, anticipation, expectation."[9] But not for long. Toward the end he was saying "night more and more surrounds me."[10]

There is something unexpected, almost illogical — as if it should not have happened — in Nietzsche's collapse into an admission of homelessness. His position all along was quite different from Dostoevsky's, as illustrated by the sophistry of Kirillov. "I must affirm my unbelief, for there's nothing higher for me than the thought that there's no God. . . . Man kept inventing God in order to live. I am the first man in history to refuse to invent God."[11] This may sound like Nietzsche, except that at no time did Nietzsche imagine that he was the first to refuse to invent God. When Kirillov goes on to say "it is my duty to make myself believe that I do not believe in God,"[12] the difference appears. We know he spoke for Dostoevsky when he added, "God has tormented me all my life."[13] At no time was Nietzsche tormented by God, at no time was he unsure of his unbelief. But he was mistaken when he thought he had the strength to endure metaphysical loneliness and at the same time the inability on the part of his closest friends to understand him.

There might seem to be a similarity between Kirillov's reluctant God and Nietzsche's free spirits and Titans of the future. The reluctant God is a man who had demonstrated his freedom by killing himself. But it never occurred to Nietzsche that these free spirits — of which he was surely one — or the new men of the future would be called upon to kill themselves. However crime and evil might be evaluated in the future, it seems not to have occurred to Nietzsche that suicide might be a necessary good. Unlike Kirillov, he had too historically oriented a mind to retreat into masochism.

Nevertheless, he arrived at a point of dangerous stillness, not only for his own life, but as a model for future generations. When we look back at him, and think of him as brother and fellow sufferer, we can forget that the void he uncovered in the mind of man remains, and that therefore it is unsafe to assume, as he did, that the seas are really open and the horizon clear. On the contrary, the dramatic literature of our time, even more than its philosophy, has made it evident that psychological nihilism is now a cultural fact so firmly established that the only way of living with it is, paradoxically, not to take it too seriously. This is the method and part of the point of the plays of Beckett and Pinter.

77 § **the void**

VARIATIONS OF NOTHINGNESS

In Beckett's plays nothing happens; in Pinter's plays things do happen, the wrong things, terrible things. For both there is "nothing certain," "nothing to be done," for everyone is "alone in the midst of nothingness."[14] It might seem that Beckett's characters are better off because even in their aimless shuffling of talk back and forth they can imagine they are Adam, made in the image of God, and can compare themselves to Christ. But the comparisons are not apt, for all they do is wait. If this is hope, as Beckett has said, it is hope based on wishful thinking rather than ministry, passion, and sacrifice. There is in Pinter much suffering, the suffering of the insulated and enclosed, living in a world where no one knows what is going on in another's mind, and where the only clues to one's own mind are recollections. These at least are often warm and loving, however distant they may be. Perhaps this is healthier, preferable to Beckett's more abstract insistence on hope where there would seem to be no point to hope. To say "I can't go on like this," and then to go on quite cheerfully, suggests that Beckett is concealing whatever it is that enables him to live a personal life which is not paralyzed by the sight of the void. Is it so simple, as his plays suggest, the old friendly hostility between head and heart, the silence of the world and the nostalgia of the human spirit? Or is there a real world to live in and think about and celebrate, as well as a metaphysical void? Marcel may have been right in insisting that we learn how to construct a concrete metaphysics, for whatever he may have meant by this, it should be possible to talk of the realities we care about and not be paralyzed by looking into the void of an impossible metaphysics.

We might imagine Beckett saying "if there is a God, I'll wait for him" and Pinter saying "if there's a God, he's not worth talking about." Sartre once said of himself, "I collared the Holy Ghost in the cellar and threw him out; atheism is a cruel and long-range affair; I think I've carried it through."[15] Smart talk speaks for itself. Beckett's waiting, however unsupported, has the same air of seriousness that the later Heidegger's has. "The holy does indeed appear," announced Heidegger, "but the god remains far off."[16] Beckett would agree to that. But he would not go so far as to speak of God's failure, and the need of man to remain near that failure. Indeed, it is difficult to make much sense of such talk. Whether God has withdrawn — and thus failed us — or whether we have failed him and ourselves is a secondary question in comparison with the suspicion that there is no God anyway, and void is his name.

Beckett's characters experience nothing and imagine something else. Pinter's remember reality and make no connections with each other. The loneliness of non-communication may in the end be no worse than the isolation of a mind that pretends reality where there is none. Hope without reality is only an excuse for not following evidence to a conclusion. That was not a mistake Camus was likely to make. He knew nothing of hope or reverberations from a distant God. He knew what men can do to each other in the name of reason, murder, betrayal, and these are worse evils than the inability of one man to know what is going on in another's mind. He did not hope; he did something better, he promised to work for a just world, in moderation, and with some kind of love for that world. He shared this affection for physical reality — including human beings — with Pinter, and carefully avoided abstractions, metaphysical or religious, unless they were in some way supported by what he knew to be possible. He did not expect justice to come to him like a returning God. He intended to go out and help bring it into the world. Compared to this attitude, there is a sterility in Beckett precisely in so far as an abstract hope matches an abstract void. There is more future — whatever the difference between future and hope may be — in a world where one is reminded of sea, sun, earth, lost loves, than in a world where nothing happens, and where nobody comes and nobody goes. To laugh at this world is to admit, with immense relief, that it is false. To laugh with Pinter is to realize that in spite of the fact that it is impossible much of the time to verify what goes on and why, things do happen, and some things are frightening, and some things are beautiful.

SOLITUDE

Laing has said that "people in our time neither experience the Presence of God, nor the Presence of his absence, but the absence of his Presence."[17] He also says that "there is everything to suggest that man experienced God."[18] However that may be, it is interesting that a study of schizophrenia can take note of the absence of Presence in the same way and to the same extent as a study of culture (Nietzsche) or a study of relationships of men and women in society (Proust). The twentieth century abounds in similar testimonies coming from different directions and disciplines. Metaphysical nihilism stands alongside "our own appalling state of alienation called normality."[19]

It would be a mistake, but not a great one, if we were to concentrate too literally on the chronology of history. Kierkegaard has nothing to say about the void, but he has plenty to say about self-isolation, which has all the earmarks of a schizophrenic sickness unto death. Not until Dostoevsky did we have a full-blown description of men who at one and the same time recognized the void and were bottled up inside themselves. In the person of Nietzsche this association became a fact, although the important thing about Nietzsche was his obsessive concentration on the void. But when we reach the twentieth century itself the examples multiply of the companionship of these two dimensions of human existence, the acknowledgment of the impossibility of transcendence and the isolation and paralysis of the individual who has given up on Presence — Kafka, Proust, Heidegger, Beckett, Ionesco, Pinter.

This is not to deny that some men and women, like Kierkegaard, go on believing in transcendence and yet remain locked up inside themselves, or that others can look into the void and still communicate with someone else. This too is part of the imbalance of a part of history to which not everyone responds consistently. There are still human beings who have not been totally disabled in one way or another. But they are few.

There is no point pushing the historical aspect of this further than to note that it is impossible to find in the literature and philosophy of any century before the nineteenth examples of a preoccupation with both ontological nihilism and schizophrenia raised to the level of a universal experience. What we now see are not exceptions. Existentialism is a historical perspective, mediated by philosophy, that has been responsive to a total tranformation of man's insight into his inner experience.

When Beckett, in his book on Proust, wrote of "that irremediable solitude to which every human being is condemned,"[20] he was, of course, not thinking only of certain categorical statements but of the long story of anguish, indifference, and betrayal that is woven into the narrative of *Remembrance of Things Past*. Proust meant to be shocking when he said, "We exist alone. Man is the creature that cannot emerge from himself, that knows his fellows only in himself; when he asserts the contrary he is lying."[21] No more frightening judgment has ever been made of human existence, not even the announcement that God is dead, for it is tantamount to saying that man is dead also.

When Proust also said that "the only true paradise is always the paradise we have lost,"[22] he was thinking of his own past, which was never as vividly present at the time as it became later on through involuntary memory. We could apply it to a lost world of religious or metaphysical absolutes to which we can return only through reading and study. It certainly is difficult now to imagine a future when man can ever again use symbols of absolutes in the same ways and for the same purposes. It is easier to believe that schizophrenia can be healed, easier because it is happening already.

When Laing, whose learning combines both psychoanalytic and existential theory, says that "the distinction between the absence of relationships and the experience of every relationship as an absence is the division between loneliness and perpetual solitude, between provisional hope or hopelessness and a permanent despair,"[23] we should be cautious not to read into the theme of absence a void so deep that it makes the human spirit disabled and isolated. He himself does not go so far, for he believes that the beginning of the road back to openness lies in sharing the absence of relationship. Perhaps we can at times do no more; perhaps it is not enough, and this is what it means to say that if we are alone with each other and each other's experience of absence, we are very alone indeed. I do not think that real presence is out of the question even now, even for those who know the experience of absence from the inside but who are wounded and not necessarily permanently disabled. The place to look for health is not only in a lost paradise, which we have kept active throughout both depression and despair, but in a far country beyond.

the
major themes

4 SELF-ISOLATION

THE GREAT DEEP

Isolation is not the last word, not even the next to the last. Whether it accompanies the discovery of the void, or whether the isolated man seems to be unaware of that dimension of existence, it is not sufficient to say that he is shut up inside himself, cannot get out to make contact with others. A life goes on inside, varied and complex, depending on the individual, but also conditioned by certain fundamental limitations of knowledge and experience. Everything one says about the self should be regarded as tentative, born in swirling mists of conflict and self-conflict. Hardly anything can be said that one is not be tempted to revise or even cancel — most of all, whatever we try to say about interior motives and directions of the soul. We use metaphors like divided self, two selves, centripetal and centrifugal, labyrinth, planes, depth, center; we should be

reminding ourselves that the entire philosophical enter-
prise is a kind of dream, much more than a science with
hypotheses which we may try out. For it is quite possible
to try out almost all these metaphorical hypotheses and
find them to some extent plausible and sometimes useful
in therapeutic experimentation. What works is not always,
however, a sure guide to what is.

This is why Augustine is on the whole a safer guide to
the human interior experience than most. He thought of
man as "a great deep,"[1] "a great question to himself."[2]
In these two images alone we can see the range of the difficulty of self-knowledge, and the challenge. Man is *grande
profundum* because he can never know all of himself. He
is *magna quaestio* because his motives and his behavior
do not follow prejudged ideals. Just as one cannot come
to the end of himself, so one cannot also find out where and
how to begin. So much seems to be out of one's hands
that we feel and behave compulsively; and the longer we
live the more we can appreciate the immensity of our past,
and the more we wonder what difference it makes to our
future whether we know much about it or not.

Augustine's story begins with his search for God and
himself, for rest, and in rest he eventually found both himself and God. At this point in our attempt to understand
the existentialist tradition, it is important to mention
memory, which is the most obvious introduction to the
identity of a man. No one has spoken more eloquently
about memory than Augustine: "the fields and spacious
palaces of memory," "this treasure house," "the great
harbor," "the huge court," "a vast and boundless subter-
ranean shrine," "this immense capacity." "Who has ever
reached the bottom of it?"; "I cannot totally grasp all that
I am"; "there is something of man that the very spirit of
man that is in him does not know"; "a man is for the most

part unknown even to himself."[3] We had better not be so moved and distracted by the eloquence that we forget the main point of it, an argument for the profoundest skepticism.

In our century Heidegger has defined man as the creature whose being it is to know himself and to know being. In some sense everyone might agree. But it would be rash to agree without tempering agreement with Augustine's sad and poignant admission of final frustration. There is always that which we can never find out, and it may well be the most important thing of all. Besides, "every man is a stranger in this life, and every heart enclosed to every other heart"[4]; "thou seest not my heart, and I do not see thine; it is night."[5] It is ironic that the impenetrability of other people to us is likely to be much more disquieting than the impenetrability of ourselves to ourselves — likely, that is, to twentieth-century man. Augustine's friendships were many and close, and isolation was not a problem for him. He did not have to discover others; he had to discover himself.

In the course of his search he had to deal with an unquiet heart, a mind that was never satisfied for long by theory, erotic compulsions, conflict between sex and self-discipline, "twisted knottiness."[6] "I became to myself a wasteland."[7] In that wasteland he gradually became unbearably tormented by a division between his desires, for lust and also for purity, "two wills, one of them not entire, one has what the other lacks." And he felt ashamed. At a certain point his tolerance of division was shattered, and he became a whole man, in control of himself. This is what we call conversion.

The recovery of himself could take place only because of the intensity of his self-conscious quest for peace and identity. Without that he would never have gained control, never come to a place of self-assurance and tranquility. It is instructive to compare his divided will with several other kinds of division. His own model might well have been St. Paul's formula: "I do not understand my own actions. For I do not do what I want, but I do the very thing I hate."[8] This is different from Dostoevsky's contradictions which exist side by side. The same man loves both Sodom and the Madonna, at one and the same time, and finds beauty in both: "They all say they hate evil, but in their heart of hearts they all love it."[9] Augustine called his moral stand-off a sickness of the soul, but Dostoevsky's fascination with evil was not a standoff but a deliberate embrace. There was nothing really compulsive about it, although it appeared so to those who did not know what was going on inside the head of the criminal, who always had his reasons, even if he changed his mind about those reasons after the fact. Evil might be done for gain, it might be done accidentally, but usually it was done to demonstrate an individual's freedom. Would he dare to exercise his freedom in this way?

Only an immature mind would mistrust itself enough to follow that route. Thus the boy Augustine stole pears he did not need. He never again had to prove his freedom by doing something that was meaningless, apart from being illicit. Dostoevsky, on the other hand, seems to have been convinced that this doubleness told something of impor-tance about nineteenth-century man, living in a "period of isolation."[10] Whether we call Raskolnikov and the Under-ground Man and Ivan and Stavroguin immature or morbid makes little difference. Condescension cannot explain them. It is better to point to the coincidence of their fascina-tion with evil, their belief that they could only be sure they were free if they did what they knew to be wrong, their in-

x) Reading "lit." as philosophy!

creasing isolation from others, their final inability to love, and, in addition, their unbelief.

This coincidence may tell nothing about causes, although to someone who walks by himself in darkness the loneliness without divinity as well as humanity may be just the extra element that could ensure paralysis. Who can tell? Nietzsche's insanity, which seems symbolically appropriate, in a bizarre way, is said to have been caused by syphilis. Dostoevsky's heroes came to their dead ends through what was then called brain fever. There was no further step for reason to take; it had already arrived, quite reasonably, at zero.

Theologians called the Pauline compulsion original sin. Augustine's sickness of soul, however Pauline in dynamic, has a universal dimension, even though it is his own special temperament. Clinical schizophrenia has both environmental and hereditary aspects. Are we really looking at three distinct phenomena? They are all destructive to the self. Are their causes very different? It is impossible to say. But when we compare Augustine with Dostoevsky's split characters and the clinically defined schizophrenics of our time, there is an element of experience present in Augustine's life that is not definitely known to be present in the lives of the latter, namely, a warm family relationship from childhood. Dostoevsky himself made much of this in *The Brothers Karamazov*, and it is probably not far-fetched to think that he knew he had missed this in his own early life. "There's nothing higher, stronger, more wholesome and more useful in life than some good memory, especially when it goes back to the days of your childhood, to the days of your life at home."[11] Of the isolates whom we call schizophrenics Laing says, "The schizophrenic is desperate, is simply without hope. I have never known a schizophrenic who could say he was loved, as a man, by God the Father or by the Mother of God or by another man. When someone says he is an unreal man or that he is dead, in all seriousness, expressing in radical terms the stark truth of his existence as he experiences it, that is — insanity."[12]

We may have no sure way of knowing whether schizophrenia is a modern social disease. It probably is not. The experience of absence of relationships in the past century does exist side by side with the cultural word that God is dead. When Great Pan died, Christ was born, and it has taken many centuries for nihilism to become complete. From a psychological point of view the experience of absence is one, whether the presence or the absence refers to God or man. From a psychological point of view it probably matters little whether one speaks of transcendence or presence, provided that both words stand for an experience of reality, and not simply an ideal soulfully longed for. The practice of presence allows one to understand the difference between isolation and transcendence; in its absence, there can only be isolation and a shrinking or false sense of personal identity.

THE LABYRINTH

I do not think Laing is fair when he says that "existential thinking offers no security, no home for the homeless."[13] His own understanding of transcendence and presence contradicts this. It is true that there is no security in the contemplation of insecurity, whether it is called alienation or self-isolation. And it is true that existentialism cannot move on to consider the possibility of presence until it has taken seriously the alienated world, both interior and exterior. No one is safe once and for all; death, chance, care-lessness, and selfishness can at any time destroy inner and interpersonal security. If this is what he means, then one would have to say, "I accept insecurity." Alienation is not our destiny nor a state from which it is impossible to be extricated. Existentialism is neither pessimistic nor optimistic. It concerns itself only with alternatives.

There are difficulties in talking about alienation or self-isolation that are not mentioned often enough. In the first place, if we were to take our view of the interior life of the alienated from Sartre, it would seem impossible not to feel trapped by his negative vision and yet suspect that Sartre himself in some mysterious way does not feel trapped. No one can be sincere, but someone, presumably Sartre, can be authentic. If we were to take our view from Kierkegaard, it would seem easy to be oneself — the very thing Sartre says one cannot be — although he makes it clear that most people, whether they realize it or not, are in a state of despair of being themselves. And yet somehow it is possible, as it was for Kierkegaard, to be himself — to be self-isolated, and yet not despair and not relate himself to the eternal without which he should, by definition, be desperate. If, on the other hand, we are impressed by the labyrinthine world of Kafka, who felt rejected, felt worthy of rejection, resisted this judgment, and was capable of laughing at his own despair and reason for despair, we might find it difficult to understand how he, conditioned for schizophrenia, could avoid its breach with reality.

These are only three alternative ways of looking at the labyrinth of an interior life that is not free for transcendence or presence and that wrestles more or less helplessly with the nature of its identity. Each has an aura of reality about its analysis, and one is tempted not to approve but to look at each instance of alienation as an illustration of the analysis that comes closest to one's own experience.

Each assumes a fairly rigid interior structure, and the longer one looks at these structures, the more one takes for granted that there really is an existential system. And then one fine morning, as Kafka would say, the neatness and order are not there any more, and all one sees is swirling vapor, and one's head spins, and one comes close to a nausea Sartre has never known, a nausea of intellectualism. This is the same reaction that Kierkegaard recorded in his own way, by a savage rejection of philosophy. The irony is that one can react to him that way too. If it were possible to keep existentialism as a tentative, provisional perspective separate from existentialism as a structured philosophy, we would not have to look forward to seeing it as ultimately denying its primary vision of experience. It probably is not possible. Vision implies order, and order suggests structure, and before one knows what has happened, the structure is equated with reality.

DESPAIR

Assuming then that the very nature of self-entanglement and isolation lends itself to alternative patterns and therefore alternative theories, it is enough to remind ourselves of some of these, without making too much of relationships or insisting that together they tell the whole story. What they should do is persuade us that it would be risky to assume that anyone can escape some form of alienation.

Most of us know that we have failed ourselves in one or more ways. Sometimes we have failed to live up to a standard set by ourselves, more often by others. Some feel an active judgment against them for not living up to a standard which may or may not be credible; then too, the judgment may or may not be fair. Some try to live with that judgment by reforming themselves, others by conforming. Some try to escape by hiding, so that they cannot be hurt again, so that they cannot even hear. Some try to escape by seeking a life and identity that will be immune from attack. Some try to break away from the judging world. Others try to defy or destroy that world. Some do not know what to do, and spin round and round aimlessly. Some think they know what is happening to them, and why. Some are utterly bewildered about the facts. Some think they know, and they do not know; we know from the outside that they do not know. Sometimes they know or think that we think we know what they do not know. Sometimes they are right, and sometimes we are.

At times we feel embattled, or in a state of siege, because we have not had time to prepare ourselves to travel out from the inner world to a world in which some strange instinct tells us we really belong. We are arrested, at the wrong time, and perhaps unfairly, while we are sorting out our problems and destiny, and are condemned for not having had enough time to do so. Sometimes we try to escape all these dangers and tribulations by simply lying, pretending to be what we certainly are not. And sometimes we demand that we be what we are, even if we do not like what we are. We try to get ahead of ourselves, and others, by thinking that we can stop time and then look back at what is finished. All we can really do is recognize that the whole landscape of the interior life is boobytrapped.

Kierkegaard, for example, thought he knew the structure of despair. He meant the state of being dissociated from one's real self, not just the unpleasant feeling accompanying that state. He believed that one's real self is not accepted until it relates itself to the eternal. He believed that many people are in despair who do not know it because they do not think of themselves in terms of anything ultimate (as untouched by boundary situations). They do not even know enough about themselves to experience their dissociation consciously, as despair. He distinguished further between two kinds of open despair, the despair of a person who does not want to be himself, who deliberately avoids developing the sense of identity and quest for identity which he is aware is open to him in some way. "The whole problem of the self becomes a sort of blind door in the background of his soul behind which there is nothing."[14] The torment of despair is that one wants to avoid oneself, and yet that very self cannot be avoided, just because it does have for itself an eternal validity. The most intense, the most lacerating kind of despair is that of the person who would like to separate himself from that eternal validity so badly that he defies it openly and refuses to move toward the very thing he cannot help believing in. This was Kierkegaard's own experience: "This despair is the sort which rarely is met with in the world. That blind door behind which there was nothing is in this case a real door, a door carefully locked to be sure, and behind it sits as it were the self and watches itself employed in filling up time with not willing to be itself, and yet is self enough to love itself."[15]

This is the despair of the strong, and it is hard for us to be sorry. And yet even the strength of the defiant can turn into a disability which becomes so habitual it is no longer a matter of choice. Then the despair makes one helpless indeed. The case of Dostoevsky's Stavroguin is of this kind. He had chosen not to choose. The difference between him and Kierkegaard is principally that instead of holding back from choosing the good of his soul, he insisted on trying everything. It is a difference of emphasis only. In appearance Stavroguin at times resembles the enigmatic watchfulness of the man who sits behind the closed door;

at other times he makes unpredictable forays into the world
of men and women, now helping, now harming. "I've tried
my strength in everything. But what was I supposed to
apply my strength to? I'm still capable of wishing to do
something decent and I derive some pleasure from this;
but the next moment I want to do evil things and that also
gives me pleasure. But neither of those wishes is strong
enough to direct me. The only thing that has come out of
me is negation without strength and without generosity."
He added, "I am also incapable of despair."[16] Nevertheless he killed himself.

The isolated man may have a firm idea of himself, yet he
will be unpredictable. He cannot predict his own course of
behavior because, as Kierkegaard tried to explain, in some
sense he does not know himself. He only knows that he
does not want to know, and this is not enough. To refuse
one must be free; refusing is a sign of freedom. It is also a
closing of doors, and a curtailment of freedom. The world
is smaller — of necessity, sometimes — when one refuses,
and therefore there is always some loss. When one has refused to press forward to the ends of his spirit, to go as far
as acceptance of the world and its mystery, he has reversed
the course of freedom and started a process which can
end in paralysis. The inner self may become untouchable
and untouched, but may also become too shrunken to be
worth living for. In one last moment of realization, the only
conclusion could be not to live. This is always the spectre
behind despair.

CONDEMNATION

The pattern of Kafka's alienation is a variation of this,
desperate in detail, high, dry, and safe when all is said and

done. He suffered, and yet some resilience, some detachment from himself — which Kierkegaard did not have — enabled him to endure his suffering. His father had seen to it that he had "lost his self-confidence and developed a boundless sense of guilt."[17] He was rejected and he knew it. He was not absolutely sure that there might not be some reason why he should be rejected, although not the unreasonable reasons his father gave. He did not choose either the way of total withdrawal or the way of rebellion. He felt his whole being needed access to some reality that had been denied him, and he could not be sure that he was worthy of such access. He lived in that shadow world between a reality which he judged unfair and possibilities the existence of which he could not prove. He avoided final judgment by accepting all possibilities. And so he got to know the despair of not choosing, and escaped its strait jacket by acceptance. Thus life for him could be both painful and comic, trapped and yet free. Only such a man could have written: "He could have resigned himself to a prison. To end as a prisoner — that could be a life's ambition. But it was a barred cage that he was in. Calmly and insolently, as if at home, the din of the world streamed out and in through the bars, the prisoner was really free, he could take part in everything, nothing that went on outside escaped him, he could simply have left the cage, the bars were yards apart, he was not even a prisoner."[18] He is like the man from the country in *The Trial* who did not dare to enter the door to the Law because he was told not to, only to find at the end of his life that this door was intended for him. Kafka suspected that this might be so, and yet he felt unable to pass through that door — at times he could not even find it.

What makes Kafka's alienation radically different from Stavrogin's — and probably from Kierkegaard's — was that he knew how to keep all possibilities open, all balls in the air. His deftness was almost superhuman. Perhaps his form of torment was also different. For although he was filled with self-doubt and mistrust, with an intense and abiding sense of worthlessness, at the same time he never broke contact with everyone around him, and he shared his inner self, in one way or another, with his friends. He was tormented but never totally isolated, never cut off from the real possibilities that other people represent and that serve to keep oneself in some perspective. Kafka's perspective must be understood not only in terms of his permanent sense of humiliation and rejection, but also in terms of an elemental toughness and humility. His sense of all possibilities was unswerving, and this caused him both torment and detachment. His humility prevented defiance from obstructing his vision, and also made him generous and affectionate.

The inner self does depend on the outer self, which, in Kafka's terminology, is the origin of judgment and suggestion. Whatever initiates the process of self-evaluation is by definition so respectable that it is taken for authority. Some authority, however misleading, it does have. It is not also the way, and this is where Kafka made his mistake, a mistake he made with open eyes. He felt he "needed to be provided at every instant with a new confirmation of his existence"[19] from the very source that, having given him existence, had also put it in question. If only he could imitate his father by marrying, then all might be well; he would have passed through the gate and escaped judgment. "It is as if a person were a prisoner, and he had not only the intention to escape, which would perhaps be attainable, but also, and indeed simultaneously, the intention to rebuild the prison as a pleasure dome for himself."[20]

But this will not work. The Law is one thing, as one person is separate from another, and the self alone is the way, both to and away from the Law and what it represents for good or for ill.[21] And we must conclude that in the absence of a certain kind of presence the self not only is the way, it is the authority as well, the only authority. But it is an authority that can be expected at worst to condemn itself, or at best to keep everything in suspension. With luck — or grace — the time may come, another authority may come, that could relieve the need for suspension and could heal.

NEGATIONS

One grows used to the equation of self-isolation and pain and to the degree of self-control that yields both analysis and metaphors. It is almost shocking to enter the Sartrean world of inner negation and conflict and to find it apparently without anguish at all and without poetry: "The human being is not only the being by whom *négatités* are disclosed in the world; he is also the one who can take negative attitudes toward himself."[22] The Sartrean vision is an extraordinary one. In the abstract it seems to be iron-clad, utterly self-enclosed and self-sufficient, without anguish, and without humor. Everyone is judged, except perhaps Sartre himself, who escapes into some place of authenticity. Nevertheless, however natural it is to resent being backed into a corner, it is hard not to admit that this adversary has reason on his side, at least up to a point. The time may come when, as in Kafka's parable of the prisoner and his cage, one finds that the bars are actually set wide enough apart for one to walk through. Sartre may have done that himself; if so, he can, in turn, be accused of bad faith toward his readers for not letting them in on his secret.

Like Heidegger, Sartre begins with attention to the nature of consciousness, but instead of remarking on its prevailing

mood of care and its constituent elements, he singles out
the distance between consciousness and that of which it is
conscious. It is possible for him to claim that consciousness
implies a lack, a separation, a detachment, a fissure, a hole,
a decompression, a deterioration, nothingness. For Sartre
it is one and the same thing to say that consciousness is "a
being the nature of which is to question its own being" and
that it is "a being the nature of which is to be conscious of
the nothingness of its being."[23] Consciousness reveals a
crisis more profound and omnipresent than any boundary
situation, namely, an uncertainty about one's relationships
to self and others.

Sartre's basic distinction between In-itself and For-
itself[24] is meant to remind us, however abstractly, that
human existence is not only unsettled, but that it is the
nature of human existence to go about the business of trying
to make and settle itself as long as it lives. The uncertainty,
the fatigue, the disillusionment accompanying this infinite
process conspire to tempt the self to stop time and crystal-
lize self at some moment of its life. But as long as there is
life there is no hope: the For-itself cannot become an In-
itself, a human being cannot, without dying, become a
thing. Nor can the human being become an In-itself–For-
itself, for that would mean it had escaped being at the
mercy of general contingency and of other people and
had become the foundation of itself. In this same sense,
not only is "man a useless passion,"[25] because he would
like to lose himself as man in order that he may become
God, but he can never establish his identity. The quest for
identity is also a useless passion because there is always a
gap between being and becoming, between what one is and
what one is to be.

Man, for Sartre, faces a double difficulty. On the one
hand he is, as Heidegger said, always ahead of himself,

never at rest, never the same. On the other hand, he is at the beck and call of contingency, the random influences of his own body and of realities external to himself. As Sartre puts it, these others contain my secret. In turn, I am the secret of others. Not only do they know things about me that I do not know about myself, more important, their existence and their actions limit and in that way help to create me. This means that the relationship between one being and another always contains an element of conflict, even if the conflict can, as most people suppose, be reduced by cooperation.[26]

To be For-itself is to be free. But to be free is to be condemned not only to exercise one's freedom but to clash with "alien freedoms," to appropriate the freedom of another, which by nature of its very existence limits one's own. In Sartre's view love itself is a game of mirrors and leads to perpetual dissatisfaction and perpetual insecurity. Just as his view of consciousness is an awareness of distance between self and self, decompression rather than plenitude, so his view of what it means to be in the world, to be with others, is to be separated, put on the spot, transfixed as by a stare, challenged, devoured. There is so much truth in Sartre's vision, even though it is negative, that it can be applied to the alienated world of the twentieth century with no difficulty at all. It is probably the secret of this century.

Whether or not Laing is to be taken seriously when he says that the schizophrenic may be doing the only healthy thing left to him when he withdraws from an alienated world outside and thus takes one step towards ultimate liberation — for which he will need help from someone who has not himself left that world — self-isolation is, on any reading, an attempt to evade the judgment of alien freedoms. Just so Tillich defines the purpose of pathological anxiety as a technique of avoiding the questions raised by existential anxiety. Even if we were not shaken by persistent anxieties, we would be so worn out by putting up with other people and their importunities that we would welcome a leave of absence from life.

Here too Sartre uncovers a dynamism more basic than pathological schizophrenia, one in daily use in areas in which the distinction between sickness and health is never raised. The schizophrenic constructs a false self to use as a mask or barrier between the outside world and the inner self. But the false self, which the inner self hates, is constructed in the image of alien values, and the inner self, not having had time to develop, imagines itself to be both free and transcendent when in fact it is neither. Thus the poignant "futility" of the "false-self system,"[27] which cannot accept insecurity and yet remains exposed to rejection. Sartre's analysis of bad faith is more extensive than this: bad faith is almost unavoidable.

If the choice is between bad faith and sincerity, then bad faith, or at least some effort to dissociate oneself from oneself, is probably unavoidable. Sartre makes out a persuasive case for the universality of this effort. Here again his insight is negative, his analysis being one of disintegration. If I deliberately say — or pretend — that I am what I am not, then I am openly trying to avoid accepting myself as I am. Lying to others is one thing; it is worse to lie to oneself, to know the truth about oneself and conceal it at the same time. This temptation is almost forced on the self by its essential instability and by the necessity to cope with the judgment of others. The easy way out seems to be to select a self that is both completely stable and morally above reproach. But this is in fact impossible, and so the attempt results in bad faith.

If, on the other hand, one does not wish to lie to oneself but to speak the truth, then a different kind of temptation appears, namely, to be what one is, whatever that may be. Just as bad faith is a state of mind, so sincerity is a demand that one makes, an impossible demand, since no one can be what he is without being either God or a thing, an In-itself–For-itself or merely an In-itself. As Sartre says, the goals of bad faith and of sincerity are the same, to put oneself out of reach. Only the way is different. The way in each case is the creation of a disintegrated self. The final result is that the self gets lost, shut up in a false understanding of its nature, and incapable of dealing freely either with itself or others.

Is there, then, no escape from the escape mechanism? Sartre, in a footnote, suggests that "self-recovery" is possible, the self-recovery which he calls "authenticity, the description of which has no place here."[28] In spite of his reluctance to describe it, it is obvious that there is only one alternative to escape and that is not to escape, but to accept insecurity. This was Kafka's way of enduring; it is not so clear that, except in theory, it is Sartre's. In real life he has played a self-righteous part that is hard to distinguish from bad faith. Whoever wishes to accept insecurity has to learn humility and live by it.

BEYOND ISOLATION

Beyond the question of self-recovery is the question of life with others. Indeed, it is not beyond it but is an integral part of it. What could it mean to recover oneself in a vacuum? The insecurity arising from the essential disintegration of the self and its conflict with others would be unendurable if the conflict were so complete that absolute isolation were forced upon it. This can happen, and does. War, revolution, illness, social rejection of one sort or another can totally oppress and totally isolate. But even in these situations other people can offer saving graces. In spite of what Sartre says, in spite of mixed motives, it must be stressed that every day people are giving to other people in such a manner that there not only is no conflict, no threat to the identity of others, but there is a strengthening. Moreover, it is possible to strengthen the identity of someone else without diminishing one's own.

Another theory is needed to describe what takes place, in spite of Sartre's cynicism. Fortunately, human existence is more diverse than any one man's vision of it, diverse, but also, to do justice to Sartre, unstable. What is missing from Sartre's vision is the reminder that consciousness is not only or primarily a consciousness of negations, but that it is a consciousness of reality, the reality of self and others. To theorize only on the basis of part of one's experience is itself an act of bad faith and insincerity. To talk about human existence from the point of view of self-isolation is to mislead others into supposing, despite their own experience, that they have no direct intuition of reality.

Interior experience, however frustrating and painful, is above all an experience of the presence of self with self, the presence of other realities along with the real self. Here we are, and there they are, present and absent at the same time. This much has to be accepted, or else an unreal pessimism or an equally unreal optimism will tyrannize the mind. Admitting this, one can still inquire about the directions of consciousness, the motions of the human spirit. In practice, individuals do behave both authentically and unauthentically, in cycles. In practice, they spend more time working out the problems of the shape of each day than they do contemplating their existence or their world in wonder and adoration. In practice, people love themselves more, on the whole, than they love anyone else, at least they think more about themselves and their imagined needs. But at times — with some people, almost all the time — they can think of others. There is a gratifying diversity in social history and individual experience, and you have to be in love with your own limited vision and your own little self to deny it. That too is part of the diversity.

One should be cautious in extrapolating any unchangeable dynamism out of all this, like assuming that a hidden God directs one's everyday life. If that were true, it might equally be true that the hidden God is camouflaged by a person's persistent search for himself. Augustine did think this, and it would be foolish to doubt that when he found God and also found himself, or found himself and found God, he was not speaking some dialectical truth about his experience. Whether God is deeper inside the self — and what, indeed, this might mean — there is no hard and fast reason for doubting that Augustine's experienece of a double recovery was real for him, and can be real for others even in our own time. In fact, the self that he finally discovered — a self tranquil after years of passionate restlessness — was one that had to be defined in terms of his openness to transcendence. This is a particular kind of self and is in its way a measure of the justification for man's belief in the reality of God. The place where all this took place was, of course, the interior experience, but an experience that had exhausted itself after a desperate twisting and turning in its search for an unknown self. The self it finally met was familiar and yet new, and Augustine felt as if he had been all along looking for something important in the wrong place. "Rest is not where you see it. Seek what you seek, but it is not where you seek it."[29]

So much is properly descriptive of the experience of being lost and then finding peace. But to know whether it is also true that "I went out of myself in the search for you, and did not find the God of my heart"[30] and that "he is inside me, deeper than the deepest recesses of my heart,"[31] one would have to pass from description of process to definition of causes and an assumption of different kinds of reality. This is metaphysics at its worst, a guessing game. Even though experience alone should be taken as trustworthy, it too often eludes our grasp. Not only do we hope that some gleam of recognition will greet our representations, we had better hope that what we think today we may still more or less think tomorrow. Even then, consistency may be another snare, the defense of a narrow perspective or an unsophisticated mind.

One must choose between an excessive caution which refuses to speak provisionally and at the same time passionately and an inner drive to extend the range of one's insight into interior experience, come what may. In this respect Augustine is still a good model for us. He was passionate and self-analytical. He knew from experience that the mind of man is both structured — in some way, not necessarily his way — and unfathomable. He knew from experience that disquietude is an indication of strange inner intentions and conflicts that can destroy a man or, if he is lucky, can flow together in a single stream between peaceful shores. He is a model, and yet he was not unique. What he was and described we too can be. How each of us describes our similar interior experiences, even in so far as they may resemble his, is another, and because of much else that we now know or suspect, a very different matter.

the
major themes

5 PRESENCE

SIMULATIONS

The theme of isolation is so strong in the existentialist tradition that it may seem arbitrary to insist that not only has there been a parallel and contrary theme from the beginning, but that it can be made to seem plausible. That theme is presence. Buber, who has much to say about this, has not helped by stating that "in the beginning is relation."[1] What beginning? In history? In personal development? That is unlikely. In order of importance? That is different. Tillich makes more sense when he says that life is estrangement most of the time but can move toward reconciliation. There are those, like Proust, who would deny even this. At the very least, we can say safely, with Laing, "the ways of losing one's way are legion."[2]

What we do know are inner tensions and conflict, insincerity and ignorance of personal motives, guilt and failure, frustration and darkness, shut-upness (to use Kierkegaard's word), the schizophrenia in all of us (Laing's treatment of the false-self system of masks and barriers), communication without communion ("he understands what I say to him, but he does not understand me").[3] We know because we experience loneliness and the daily efforts to avoid loneliness. We know demands, pressures, speeds that give us no time or breath to assimilate the undifferentiated particles of reality that fly by: people, events, words, weather, moods, ideas, changes of all sorts.

When we are reminded, by Pascal, that "we thoughtlessly overlook that which alone exists (the present),"[4] we admit that it is true but complain that we have no choice, because we have no time. We do not know how to use time, and so we say we have no time, shifting the blame to other realities which we now feel no one is able to deal with adequately. More and more modern man has come to think himself a victim of circumstances, as in some sense he undoubtedly is. "The present is generally painful to us. We conceal it from our sight."[5] The force of these lines is so strong that one might be tempted to think that Pascal did not believe it possible for man to experience the present at all. Whether he did or did not, many others have, above all Proust.

Proust was haunted by a dream of presence, "the idea of existence,"[6] but he firmly and sadly rejected the reality and substituted what might be called simulated presence. His own experience told him that there is an "inevitable law which only allows us to imagine that which is absent."[7] He had not experienced the present apart from instants recovered from the past through spontaneous recollection, and he did not suppose anyone else had either. He seems to have known or believed nothing, even from his reading, of the claims of other men and women, lovers or mystics.

He said flatly, "reality disappointed me,"[8] and constructed a system of fictional-autobiographical recovery of a total past which he was convinced he had not been able to taste when it was present. To him it seemed obvious that in order to apprehend and enjoy the present one would have to stop time, that time could not be stopped, that experience could be restored and be felt again, "real without being actual,"[9] "outside time."[10]

His testimony is powerful and persuasive, most of all because it conforms so exactly to our own experience — that is, in our usual state of existential isolation. Whatever the original meaning of a line Laing attributes to Heidegger, "the dreadful has already happened," it seems only too true that much that is dreadful has already happened and still reverberates, leaving the interior man vulnerable and quivering, in a bad state of nerves, and that we have had little practice in the search for an experience of presence to offset the kind of experience behind Proust's conviction. Proust's own solution is true to experience, impressive in its illustrative scope, but also desperately poignant, for it contains no hope of genuine contemplation of the present or of interpersonal sharing. Nothing he knew cancels or even questions his two primary negative propositions: "man cannot emerge from himself" and "the only true paradise is the paradise we have lost." What we have lost we have never really had.

A simulation of presence, real without being actual, is second-hand reality and takes place wholly within the mind, in complete solitude, if not loneliness. We have known people and done things with them but never had time to take in what we knew, what we could know, what was to be known. In fact, we could not manage to experience anything or anybody as a unitary phenomenon of essence and existence, *what* and *that*, *who* and *that*. So rushed are we that we concentrate either on who and what a being is or just on the fact that something or somebody is here. By the time we are ready to ask for more or see more, something else has come along and distracted us or the first being has disappeared. Besides, we are constantly engaged at working over the vast accumulation of experience, guarded by memory, active and in reserve, sorting out and relating each to each and each piece and particle to ourselves. We cannot keep up, except by arbitrarily cutting down on the pressures or withdrawing altogether to some inner cell.

The Proustian alternative to resigning oneself to a life without the present fully experienced is not the only one. Another simulation of presence, the mystical, should be mentioned. A distinction can be made between a mysticism which claims to experience reality beneath, within, or beyond sensible reality and that which aims only to experience reality as unitary within time and nature. This distinction, which must be carefully preserved, is between Christian and Zen mysticism, or, to use a more functional term, contemplation. Without judging the credibility of Christian contemplation, it can at least be said that when a man says he experiences the presence of God, he is not talking of a reality that can be verified — if it can be verified at all — in the same way that his experience of another human being can be verified or shared.

Strictly speaking, it may be unfair to speak of Christian mysticism as simulation of presence, using the theological imagination in a way parallel to Proust's use of involuntary memory; one might be content to say that with or without a conscious belief in an experience of God, the problem of experiencing moment after moment of sensible reality remains as a separate possibility in its own right, and for most people it is the main problem. In this way Zen is closer to existentialism than to Christian contemplation (not to be confused with Christian moral experience). It is also closer than the claim of Buber that "in each Thou we address the eternal Thou."[11] It is not altogether clear what Buber means by "the eternal Thou," in any case, and whether it makes any difference to the main thrust of his insight into the practice of real presence between people, or between people and nature. The term "eternal Thou," like God, for which it is probably a synonym, is introduced without much amplification and intrudes upon an otherwise plausible presentation of alternative modes of experience that require faith beyond knowledge.

Those who divide existentialists into two kinds, the religious and the non-religious, have a strong case, in so far as they wish to separate descriptions of experience from theories of experience. It does not help for a believer to say that he experiences God and that he is as entitled to call his theory a description as the next man. He does not mean the same thing by the word experience, for even he does not think of his experience of God as of the same order as his experience of himself, of other people, of nature or artifacts. His experience of God is an additional thing, within, beneath, beyond all those more immediate realities. Nevertheless, we should not emphasize this difference between the religious and non-religious existentialists to such an extent that we ignore their common effort to move toward a practice of presence that is open to all men who are not, as Marcel puts it, "encumbered with themselves"[12] and therefore temporarily incapable of presence. What should be temporary can be made permanent by habit and in the absence of help.

It is not accidental that both Buber and Marcel are inheritors of the biblical tradition. They believe in God, and their persuasion that presence is possible between men, as between men and God, is a central part of that tradition. Indeed, it would be possible — but this is not the place to attempt it — to make a case for the idea that thinking about God, even experience of God, is, as Feuerbach, an unbeliever, thought, a reflection or projection of human experience. It is also too often and too plainly a substitute for that experience. In the end, what probably matters is the quality of presence — intimacy and justice — not hypotheses about its origin. A religious person who knows no more of interpersonal presence than Proust is no better off with his practice of the presence of God than Proust was with his recollections. One kind of isolation can be as disabling as another.

There can hardly be an argument as to whether security is better than insecurity, autonomy than victimization, living in the present than living only in memory or imagination. The practical questions are not these: they are, first, whether one can choose between these alternatives (Proust thought we cannot), and second, what the shape of security is. The question is not whether we should like to have a center and not be scattered but whether it is possible to be centered; not whether we would like to live ecstatically or in union with others but whether ecstasy or communion are real options; not whether we are capable of passion but what kind of passion, the force to break through our frustrations or the compelling intention to seek the place and time to be ourselves. The question really is what it would mean to be ourselves, which is clearly different from the existential alienation that we have been describing. Anyone who says he wants to be loved for his real self, his whole self, is at least supposing that there might be something more to love than what is already taken for granted by others. He may, of course, be like the schizophrenic who only wishes there were some real inner self but who has not yet made or found one. And yet the very wish is an indication of a sense of loss and, accordingly, a mark of a central quest in human experience.

TRANSCENDENCE

Beyond the distinction between authentic and inauthentic experience is the distinction between one kind of authenticity and another. Self-isolation can also be authentic, deliberately chosen and accepted with full understanding of its consequences. It includes a conviction that any form of transcendence is impossible with man, nature, or God. It is arguable to what extent the twentieth century has laid equal restraints on man's capability for transcedence toward God as well as toward man, or whether they go hand in hand. What is scarcely arguable is that the ways by which man locks himself up in the twentieth century, and breaks out only to insult or destroy, are legion.

We should have no illusions, no false hopes, about the possibility of avoiding tragedy. No practice of presence can prevent separation by death. And the practice of presence is never immune from inner failure. There is nothing permanent about human physical presence. This is not to say, on the other hand, that human existence is so subject to time that Proust is right. On the contrary, his view of time is itself a product of a certain kind of experience, that of estrangement. A view of time coming out of an experience of presence can be quite different. Time and change are only important when loss, separation, absence, or despair of change is involved. Otherwise, we do not mind change, or in some respects, we don't even notice it. When we are doing something with someone we care for and who cares for us, it is possible for this experience to be so strong that it overwhelms the concurrent observation of change or the prospect of parting. For a while there is no time. The same is true of some of our experiences of art and nature. There is so much testimony to this effect in literature that the only real problem is that of sorting out the categories and themes and presenting them in such a way that they stand as a plausible counterpart to the world of isolation and separation.

There are two actually experienced worlds, subjectively considered: the world of being shut up in oneself and the world of being open to reality, so open that reality can break in without breaking us up. In short, this is a world defined as the real present, longed for, given, accepted, joined, loved, secure, satisfying the whole man. But if in weariness or despair one's self-confidence erodes, the first stage, waiting, will seem useless. And yet, if waiting seems worth trying, then one waits either for some sign of recognition or, if one is lucky, for actual consummation. In a time of loneliness and homelessness, waiting is a fragile affair, unauthorized by anything more than a radical determination of the inner center of the self not to be permanently enclosed.

In a life where failure has been a vivid experience, where rejection has also reached into the defenses and slashed around there, nostalgia for a different kind of life may also be in danger of being washed away by despair. No presence is possible simply by wishing for it. Presence requires two elements, some person or event (even in nature) that complements the wishing and seeking. If one is ever to move, in the contemplative spiral arising from the center of one's identity, from nostalgia to union, one has to be given the chance to pass beyond the focal point of recognition and acceptance. It cannot be denied that presence does depend to a great extent on chance. There is no such thing, contrary to Proust's strange hope, as "perpetual adoration." There is not even a guarantee of any adoration at all. In the twentieth century there is apparently no guarantee of nostalgia either, so encumbered and lonely are we all.

What is at stake is an appreciation of reality of any kind in our time. To what extent and how do we seek it, remember it, long for it, meet it? How much do we know of experiences of transcendence such as being recognized and accepted, or accepting ourselves or others, of longing, of being glad and grateful, of adoration, of union, of peace, security, and the sense of meaning that comes from complete satisfaction? These are fair questions, and the answers have been coming in for some time, yet there are those who really seem to know nothing of any of these things, or will not speak of them. Others seem to know them all. Still others are traveling the road in between and do not know because they have not experienced the whole course. The main thing is that no one be so imprudent as to exclude that which he himself has not yet come to.

Philosophers can be as skeptical as they please about the adequacy of the terminology used to point to aspects of experience. It is not adequate, and no existential philosopher, remembering Kierkegaard's cautions about abstractions, should ever be tempted to think he can encapsulate what has happened in what he writes. All that he can hope for is that what he writes may evoke some recognition in others. He knows that "presence," "recognition," "sharing," "union," "meeting," "relation" are words with many other uses from other contexts. He knows that he must surround his main terms with what gives them their special significance. He hopes and expects that those who read or listen to him will try to trace the connections between the features, see the whole face, and then relate it to other faces of reality that they have known.

SCANNING AND MEETING

Buber has said that "only he who believes in the world is given power to enter into dealings with it. . . . if only we venture to surround it with the arms of our spirit, our hands will meet hands that grip them."[13] Even if we have some inkling of what he means — for this is a highly personalized way of talking about experience — we not only must contend with the constraints of history but with philosophical skepticism as well. Laing, who has tried to restore the meaning of presence within psychotherapy, talks like a phenomenologist when he says "consciousness is a scanning mechanism."[14] Is it only that, or can it be, is it at all times, to some degree, an experience of presence? Is our awareness of ourselves, the hills and fields and sky, music, painting, other persons, scanned, or is it felt as present? There is a difference between the scanner, which sweeps across points of reality without stopping or identifying them, and the eye, inner or outer, which rests, however briefly, firmly and with concentrated attention on someone or something. There is a difference also in the effects of the gaze — whether the result of the experience "reveals me to myself . . . makes me more fully myself,"[15] as Marcel has said of presence, or whether it simply provides me with data which I can use if I wish.

Buber has reversed the natural order. One does not first believe in the world and then go out to meet it. The world has to come to us before we can believe in it. And of course the world is around us all the time. Does the one mean anything more than the other? In practical terms it does, for it is no use telling someone who is locked up inside himself that he should unlock himself and get out, that there is a world outside waiting for him to embrace. The world has to do more than wait; it has to break in in some way in order to spring the prisoner. In theology this activity is called grace. Only when it takes place is the recipient assured, without confusion or doubt, of his reality, vitality, autonomy, and identity. The wish to be "palpable"[16] is a metaphor for this inner core of self-assurance. Unless this core is established, it is no use expecting anything natural, spontaneous, or creative to flow out. Man not only cannot create anything else, he cannot create himself, until he has been given some sure sign of recognition from without, and for some men one sign is not good enough — it must be confirmed again and again and in different ways. For others, one glimpse is enough to engrave assurance on memory, and thus guarantee the dignity of nostalgia. Long before meaning is assured, nostalgia, the way to meaning, has to be confirmed.

Perhaps mystical experience, Christian or other, has been able to generate a certain momentum and life of its own once it has been touched by some kind of grace, some encounter with reality beyond the interior experience but speaking to it. It may take very little to charge the capacity for reverberating presence within the interior life. This should still not be confused with an experience of others that is continuing and reciprocal. When Simone Weil talks of spending her life waiting for "the compulsion of God's presence,"[17] she is not excusing herself from taking a step toward God. Rather, she is recognizing that it is no use trying to take a step toward anything unless there is evidence of readiness on the other side. This readiness cannot be proved by pious truisms such as "God is always ready." No one can become a "true self" without the encouragement of others. Identity depends on presence, on being singled out.

THE MARKS OF PRESENCE

The experience of presence is a delicate thing, even apart from the obstacles surrounding its attainment and the ever-present danger of its foundering. Like a sea anemone it closes when handled, and when one next looks it is only a hard little shell. Everything about it is unexpected, which carries not only the negative implication that it can collapse but, even more, the uncertain but nevertheless exciting promise of inexhaustible riches. Whoever is closed and more or less out of touch with others, alienated, confused, troubled, lives a life oscillating between the self as calculator and the self as victim. In either case, the experience of reality is of separation, standoff, not union or presence. Until isolation is broken up and its self-generating dynamism converted into an openess to reality, the actual content of experience will itself be held apart in the mind as something which one has had and known but which has not transformed the personality in any major way.

Grace is necessary, a move from the outside, a gift, a waiting, welcoming presence of another. Even this is no guarantee if it is unnoticed or rejected. There is some point, therapeutically speaking, to saying that reality must be patient. From the point of view of someone who would help another, the unexpected can always happen, but one cannot count on it either. From the point of view of self-isolation, the unexpected is just an abstraction beyond experience. The sameness that the self-isolated person endures keeps him outside the knowledge of what it is like to be spontaneous. Spontaneity is not another word for freedom of choice; it is the mark of novelty which accompanies a widening of options beyond what one is accustomed to. A spontaneous person surprises himself as well as others, as he reveals his ability to respond freshly to the offerings of reality.

No possible aspect of experience is more exciting than the discovery that human existence is such that it seems as if almost anything can happen. The sense of liberation from being hemmed in by probabilities and certainties is a sure sign that one is firmly persuaded of the possibility of experiencing presence. It is not just the threshold of presence, it is part of some initial experience of presence. Whatever the mind must do to photograph all the faces of this experience, it should not be supposed that it is anything but a unitary phenomenon. Everything happens at once, although it will be some time before one understands what it all means.

The experience of presence begins when a breakthrough into the waiting inner self occurs. This takes place only by grace of something or someone else, usually unexpectedly. Both Augustine and Buber have emphasized this, the former by saying that we look for self and God in the wrong places, the latter by saying that we will not find God by seeking but rather that God will find us. This second statement should not be taken literally. Unless there is readiness on our side, it makes no sense to talk of anyone's finding us; we would remain isolated and unknowing. The nature of this readiness is another matter, and one can speculate that there is in most men, unless they are utterly disabled, some natural readiness that, given favorable conditions, will seek recognition and acceptance. To be a person is to look for a person, first to confirm one's own reality and identity and next to set up a relationship of mutual fulfillment.

To be a person is also to be capable of exercising one's whole being at once. On the one hand, a person, as opposed to an isolate, is so unencumbered that he can freely give himself, without reserve and with passion, to his experience of others. He receives from them, if they give in the same way, a power which will surprise him, unless he has known it before — the power to be himself more authentically than ever. Far from feeling beholden and therefore possessed, he will feel beholden and therefore grateful. This is totally outside the Sartrean view of life. But it is not just a view, it is a matter of record.

Whether we speak of reciprocity, sharing, availability, responsiveness, responsibility, or mutual trust and fidelity, we are talking about a closeness that is both concentrated and open. The saying "love sees with new eyes" is counterbalanced by the saying "love blinds." Both are true. But they are speaking from two different experiences of love. Where there are reserves and no reciprocity, there can be no inclusion of the rest of the world; reality narrows, clamps down, closes, and one is returned to the isolation from which he came. With total sharing come the dividends of a continuing series of experiences of presence with the rest of one's world. It is an absolute condition of presence that "the whole being" meet the world. We must trust the world first, and even before that, the world must accept us as we are or know we can be.

Only one who can say "I want what you want" and knows that the other is saying that of him is justified in saying, with the Song of Songs, "How beautiful you are, how right it is to love you."[18] This is the model for any interpersonal experience of presence, and, except by partial analogy, only interpersonal experience can grow into real presence. Nature is comparatively passive, reinforcing our use of solitude rather than extending the discovery of the self. Solitude is the stage of life when a surplus of presence can be stored away so as to condition the inner self for more. Nature's passivity with regard to what and who we are can provide the stillness so essential to the incorporation of what we have shared with other persons, but nature does not disclose us fully to ourselves. For that, there has to be an equality of being.

TIME

There is a curious fact about time in this connection. It is plain that we need time to pass in order to make our discoveries secure. And yet time is not central to our lives, except when we are prevented from living in the present. Camus has said that love is the image of man's condition without future. We know this is too often true. What we take for love does not last, but we treat it as if it would. Camus may also have meant that in love time is not an issue at all because nostalgia and desire have been transfigured into loving presence, where there is no separation of any importance. Instead, there is a fullness of realization of all things as open and possible, with no limits on insight and satisfaction.[19] This is how security would have to be described.

Kierkegaard claimed that laughter is a mark of the religious dimension of life. If that means a dimension of life where full acceptance is taking place, then it is easy enough to conceive a security that gives one the liberty to laugh. Nietzsche's joyful widsom, like Kierkegaard's sense of the ridiculous, was, unfortunately, marred by an unremitting and painful isolation. But the instinct for liberation and laughter was, nevertheless, genuine. There is sense in the proposition that the more secure we are the more we are able to laugh. I think the only security worth waiting for is the security of presence. In the experience of mutual presence — a redundant phrase — there is meaning and satisfaction beyond the troublesome questions of why, how, when, beyond rejection and self-isolation, that old maze of insecurity worked over so diligently by the existentialists that some forgot their own personal experiences of release and confirmation in the process. A philosopher has an obligation to see that nothing real, or at least nothing he knows to be possible, is excluded. As Kierkegaard said, the philosopher must be first a whole man, and he must know what he is talking about.

afterword:

A VIEW FROM

A PARALLEL TRACK

This book was intended merely to present a coherent picture of the major existential themes found in interior experience. But I may inadvertently have done more than this by writing in the first person. If the result is that I have failed in this intention, then I am indeed sorry, but if it means, as an old friend, the poet F. T. Prince, once wrote me, that every book I write is really the same book, then whether I speak of the "existential" or not, I should be content to achieve the specific intention of each book and at the same time satisfy a need to say something about my own interior experience.

From this point of view I must admit that I always feel let down when I have finished writing, not simply because I wish that I had written more clearly and less abstractly but because I am sure that I have left something important out. One writes what one is ready to say at the time. It takes time to have anything at all to say. It takes a lifetime to say something worth rereading, for it takes time to become reconciled to the imperfect persons we are.

All my adult life I have thought what Augustine, Pascal, and many others thought. I have spoken their words, so that by now, whether by quotation or paraphrase, the sum of me may look like the sum of my selection of them. I have done this because I needed them to round out my life. My experience both preceded and followed reading and thinking about them. They taught me, but I was ready for what they taught. I have never minded acknowledging debts, which are all the lighter because I knew that I had been learning outside books as well, learning things my masters did not, perhaps could not, teach me. My life, my experience, is not exhausted by my books. More than that, the scope of my daily inner life cannot be adequately suggested by anything I have written so far. It probably should not be.

THE PERSONAL CENTER

I have wanted to write some kind of "afterword" in order to refer what I have said in other books to a common perspective and to be honest about what I myself take to be the limitations of this particular excursion into interior experience. As a pastor there are times when I am asked to try to fix in words the personality of someone who has just died, to try to recapture for family and friends something of the manner of the man. It takes a good deal of nerve to attempt this, and were it not for the emotional atmosphere of a burial service, few of us could get away with it. When it is all over, I feel I have done my best only to camouflage his memory once for all. And yet impossible as such a labor is, it is imperative that while living each of us attempt something of the sort for ourselves. But can we ever reach a level, a center, deeper than the memories and characteristic themes in terms of which our minds habitually function? Is there perhaps a third self beyond the coherence of memory and idea?

On the one hand, we are always living in the moment beyond the moments seized in insight — and distilled in words — and foolish the philosopher who in repeating himself begins to assume that he is complete, rounded out, fulfilled. A difference between a live man and a dead one not to be overlooked is that the former, making some use of his distilled ideas but of something else as well, is constantly responding to people and situations and to his own moods in ways which make him so singular that any coherent view of his ideas might never suggest the person known all too well to everyone who sees him. In contrast, something of importance in each of us seems to escape self-expression, even self-knowledge, and yet may be visible to everyone else. To come to realize this without at the same time being able to say what it is is a disconcerting discovery, but not to make it at all would condemn us to a significant kind of ignorance.

How little there is that defines a person's uniqueness. Even the most complex personalities often find to their disillusionment that almost everything they can say about themselves can be said of others. I have sometimes asked myself whether my actual interior experience coincides with the interior experience that I can put in a coherent order from the bits and pieces of familiar existentialist thinkers. Am I using them to present a vicarious portrait of myself, one not requiring an imagining of my third self? I think it likely that this is so. I am sometimes tempted to say "If I am not able to speak for myself, will somebody else, please, tell me who I am?" But who is not wary of that source of wisdom, all of us having at some time or other been forced to listen to distorted summaries of ourselves? And yet a sympathetic listener can reveal a fragment of our appearance that is invisible from within.

Exploration of the interior life begins properly with memories and themes. In fact, you do not have to be a historian to say that unless you know certain salient, however deliberately suppressed, facts about a person, you will never understand his certainties. It is not only because we find indiscretion distasteful that we withhold certain facts about ourselves, but also because we suspect — or hope — that in the end we must be judged by what we are, not by what we have done. We have our memories, but others will have to be satisfied with the conclusions we have come to; what rises to the surface may be less than what is underneath, but in the end we are going to be judged by what can be seen and heard.

CHANGES

Moreover, there are memories of quite a different kind that we should cultivate and have the courage to admit, or perhaps I should say stay loose enough to admit. I do not know whether most people's understanding of life changes as they grow older. Mine has, and will probably continue to. What really matters is that for sensitive, reflective human beings the way they once looked at life is usually no longer good enough. I can illustrate that in my own case by saying that I have always been disposed to see reality in terms of opposites (dialectically, I called it when I was eighteen and under the influence of Hegel). I have not changed in that respect. But what I used to call the dialectic (or philosophical) and the aesthetic (or poetic), I now less abstractly call the word and the flesh. The change is greater than that, however; I have come to see reality not so much in terms of apprehensions of reality as in terms of two kinds of experience, two realities.

More important, I once thought that existence is essentially the frustrating of one's deepest longings. I dreamed — metaphysical as well as romantic dreams — but I never dreamed that my dreams would come true. For many years I saw my life in nostalgic terms: I was homesick for an exexperience — whatever it might be — that would not be shattered by any manner of absence. For me life was an exile from paradise and imagination a journey to a paradise that had never been lost because, except in the imagination, it had never existed and never could exist. I found plenty of respectable reasons and models for feeling this way.

But one does not just grow older, one sometimes has a chance to see life differently. I came to understand that for some of us there are passages from isolation and nostalgia to communion and satisfaction. I finally believed what I had read many times and in many places but had not taken in because I had seen no evidence to convince me that it was not just a story. There was a time when it was normal for me to look forward with pleasurable anticipation to all sorts of things, and each time to feel let down. Much later I learned, not only how not to expect more than I would be given but to be surprised that I was being given more than I had either desired or deserved. A revolution occurred when I realized that my inner life was no longer defined by nostalgia but had been transformed, and must henceforth be defined quite differently. The nostalgic man says "I dream of. . . ." The confident man says "I can't believe it, and yet I do."

QUEST

But what kind of man will one be if he is without nostalgia? Is there ever a time when we no longer need it? It depends, of course, on how high your sights are set. Everyone needs approval and recognition for the good that he has won. Our sense of identity is confirmed, even defined, to some degree, by the names that others call us. To be occupied with the quest for identity may not be on the surface of every mind, but no one lives a day without doing something that advances or retards this search. No wonder, when the search does not go well, and uneasiness is succeeded by sheer panic or the immobility of depression. Will we ever find ourselves? Will we ever deserve to be praised? Even to be accepted blindly, and for what we know well we are not, is better than to be ignored altogether.

We have to be taught that security, the kind that can survive repeated reminders of insecurity, is possible. Unfortunately, there are no shortcuts through books, or other minds, that can put that across. If you believe someone else's conclusions — even when they are conclusions drawn from his own experience — you are still not safe from a manic attack out of the real world, that world I call the world of the flesh. Nothing is final but love, not even love's body. And words are the most fugitive of all. Anyone who has tried as often as a pastor must to reach across the ditch of grief will remember the self-disgust that followed each effort to comfort with words. Consoling words are so often words from another village. It is better just to be on hand when you are needed.

Words are important, as important as flesh. The mind that does not insist on working its way through the tough briars of experience is a mind that will surely end by falsifying experience, telling itself lies right and left and not giving a damn. I can understand little and that not well enough, but I must try to understand, casting off what makes no sense, singling out the likeliest way to keep in touch with the place from which we came. One must never lose touch with the few sources of one's life — there are not many.

In my own case, I have tried again and again to get near my beginnings by concentrating on different angles of my vision: nostalgia and presence, solitude and homelessness, love, tragedy, the dark night, the world of the thriller. Each day, in going about parish and school work, in my university teaching, as I do a variety of trivial but necessary things, I chisel and pare what I think I already know. When all is said and done, I have to admit that practically all I am is secondhand. Who then am I? I am the one who lives between two poles; I am the one who has come to call his opposites by different names; I am the one who has been completely dependent on other minds for even as incomplete a vision as I do have. Is there anything left over that is me? Is there possibly a view from a parallel track, parallel to my sight through the eyes of others? Has the mind that has understood human experience, including its own, in existentialist, religious, or psychological terms any perspective of its own? And does it matter?

With a tremor of fear I ask this. And I answer, "Yes, it does matter." I answer not only for myself but for others, like the friends I try to bring to life again in words and memory. It does matter. Each of us is different, some of us are more different. Are we different as thinkers as well? That is another question, and one we must be extra careful in answering.

THE PHILOSOPHER

Wittgenstein once said, "The difficulty in philosophy is to say no more than we know."[1] That is true, in the sense that we are always using terms that overlap, words that say more and sometimes quite different things from what we mean. But Wittgenstein did not say enough. The difficulty with most philosophers, including Wittgenstein, is that they have not said what they do know, not nearly. (On the other hand, I suppose that some philosophers know even less than they say.)

To be an existentialist one does have to have had some experience of life beyond the bland and conventional and to have reflected on it against the backdrop of the collected wisdom of the past. The reason I have never been able to identify myself with other philosophers, no matter how much I had borrowed from them, is that I always noticed with disillusionment that, like me, they had not always, at some critical point, taken the trouble to check their arguments against experience. Not only is no one infallible; worse, no one is complete.

An existentialist is one who should know one thing well, himself, as one who measures his experience against the categories of his own and other people's insights. He has a necessity, a vocation, to raise his own life to the level of some high generality. This makes him a seeker first, an analyst second, or, to put it differently, he analyzes not because he seeks release but because he seeks wisdom. There is really no substitute for this ancient definition of a philosopher, and it is a sign of cultural and individual failure when men agree to settle for less. Thinking and writing are not only ways of living, not only ways of lasting, they represent breakthroughs of the individual spirit to a plane of understanding that other people reach from their corners at about the same time. There is nothing more satisfying than to hear someone else say "Yes, I know what you mean."

Having said this, I must retreat a little, and admit that writing is no substitute for living and that a man is always more important than his books. This does not mean that a philosopher need be entirely different from his philosophy. On the contrary, one of his aims should be to leave as small a gap as he can between the two. But no matter how adequate one's insights are to one's sense of what is real, much must be left out. Memory and desire and anxiety are central facts of life, and they affect, one way or another, everything we think. In the end, it is what we think that counts, not where the thoughts have come from. We may suppress parts of ourselves — a gallery of landscapes, portraits, happenings, — so as not to embarrass others as well as ourselves. The sounds, scents, dreams, and nightmares that make up the only slightly suppressed continuum of awareness affect the quality of our responses too, but we are under no obligation to reveal them to everyone. Indeed, they usually distract us from the quest, or from the truth of our conclusions. When convictions serve to reinforce a feeling of security without at the same time encouraging illusions, their truth is sufficient unto itself.

THE PHILOSOPHER AND HIS LIFE

I know a great deal about the relationship of the things I have done to the ideas I cherish, and I see no reason why I should try to prove that my ideas are made plausible by my life. But I have never been able to make up my mind about the relevance of one part of my life to the rest, and therefore I bring it up now. I am both a pastor and a teacher, a pastor and a philosopher, and I often wonder whether thirteen years as a country parson has made an appreciable difference to my philosophical point of view. When I became a clergyman in middle life I had already been an existentialist for twenty years. I was then and am now a reluctant pastor, partly because by the usual standards for Christian ministry, standards I respect, I have felt inadequate, and partly because in our time these standards do not always meet the expectations of the laity. All this would be better left unsaid except that I suspect that in spite of the tension between my vocations, without this double experience my philosophical reflections would be even more abstract than they now are. I may be wrong. I may have kept my life in sealed compartments, and it may be only a coincidence that my mistrust of abstract argument has had to live side by side with a distaste for gregariousness. Or it may be that the passion for the concrete that I have always had has been both nourished and threatened by the kind of life a clergyman must lead.

I have always been amused by Kierkegaard's daydream of finishing his mission to Denmark and then retiring to a quiet country parsonage, but I do find myself thinking that although it might have done him no good (for he knew people pretty well already) I would not be the same man or mind had I not spent thirteen years in one parish. I have tried to imagine what a year there would do to Sartre or Heidegger — it is an amusing way of passing an idle moment — and I get no further than saying — "Not one year, thirteen!" And, recalling that Nietzsche was also a parson's son, I wonder why I see so little evidence in his works of some of the things I think I learned from my own father as I accompanied him on his parish visits to the sick and bereaved and listened to his confidences about difficult people. In the end though, most of what I learned I learned from my own mistakes and from the suffering and the gratitude of others.

It is only when I turn to philosophers from whom I have learned so much, religious philosophers and existentialists, that I observe with bewilderment that they appear not to know at all some of the things I have never been able to forget. I miss in them a certain tentativeness, a willingness to say one had not got it straight before and now has to start all over. Augustine is the only philosopher I know who ever issued a book of retractions. I miss the kind of self-confidence that permits one to say that anything can happen, the kick in the shins but also the gratitude and approval. To a pastor nothing human is ever very surprising. A good philosopher should think in the same way. Too many philosophers have boxed in both themselves and their camp followers, so that they cannot appreciate anything but some theory that excludes all the others. It does seem to make thinking easier, but how boring it makes life. The full range and sweep of human possibility is utterly open and infinite. Would that we could live forever, at the height of our powers, to take it in. But this, unfortunately, we cannot do. Even the poor philosopher must die, and he does not know whether he will be cut off in his prime one day or pared away bone by bone until one day the last organic part ceases to function and he is no more a man. The sense of urgency that undergirds a lifelong quest, the sense of mystery surrounding the complexity of both thinking and encounters with others, can keep a philosopher from taking his work too seriously. The parson in me would like to know whether Heidegger or Sartre had ever seen anything inadequate in their vision of life. Were they free enough to?

In truth, the same man who can once in a while laugh — and once in a great while laugh at himself — should be the man who has a life-long guilt about wasting his life and talents. Where have all our moments gone? Is there enough time left to capture the partly heard melody and complete it? An appealing side to Wittgenstein was his belief that he really was not even much good as a teacher. And yet at other times he thought he had said all that could be said about philosophy. What a contradiction, what a real man! A man of tensions and anguish, who at the end could say "Tell them I've had a wonderful life."[2]

I once had a nightmare in which I was in a palace of a building, a college, a seminary, I don't know which, with no one I knew, wanting to get out, wanting above all to telephone to someone I knew who cared for me. There was a telephone in every room, and each phone was on an inside line; there was no way of phoning outside the building. I have other nightmares, professional ones, like trying to conduct a church service without the right prayer book, or preaching to a congregation that is leaving one by one and talking loudly on the way out. But I have made peace with my nightmares, and no longer fear them. It is possible to live for years vulnerable to panic and demoralization, subject to depressions as well as the victim of non-recognition, real or fancied. We fear our own failure even more than we shrink from the indifference of those we would help or need. My point is not that life has much darkness — that is undeniable — my point is that a philosopher who does not live in isolation from the sensibility of others will learn in time that life has light and warmth as well as darkness and cold.

Perhaps it would be enough if the philosopher asked "Could it be that they too are right?" "Could it be that I have settled for a part of the truth and asked others to call it the whole?" It could be, and usually is. Not only must we ruthlessly discard what we do not need, as a housewife cleans out a closet of old clothes — we must discard what excludes others from heaven. How right Camus was when he said, "Nothing is true that forces one to exclude."[3] The passion for truth is a will-o'-the-wisp if it is not indistinguishable from a passion for today's experience as well as for memory and desire.

THE PHILOSOPHER AND HIS IDEAS

The good philosopher is never satisfied with what he has already said, or the good man with what he has already become. Rejection has a certain authority. When someone else rejects me, I must face, one way or another, the possibility that I am not worth paying attention to. Whoever has doubts about himself should temper his convictions and conclusions by these doubts.

The way to wisdom does not lie mainly through the things one discards, but through the deep, unswerving passion for the truth about reality, broad or narrow. Insight follows quest. What we need to come to terms with is the elusiveness of the good dream. This, our dream, is what is worth our remembering and offering to someone else. It can only be finished with another's help.

It takes so long to accumulate one's working ideas, mainly because it takes so long to have enough experience to sort out. Aristotle was right, young men cannot be philosophers; they have not lived long enough. When you have lived most of your life, you will probably have to agree with Camus also that "we live with a few familiar ideas — two or three. We polish and transform them according to the societies and the men we happen to meet. It takes ten years to have an idea that is really one's own."[4] Lucky the man who has one in ten years. Then he may find that he does not need it any more, as, for a time, I thought I no longer needed nostalgia. But what would a man do who could not dream?

I have written some books. I have been, on the whole, consistent. The same person seems to appear in each book in spite of changes of emphasis, important changes. But each time I write, each time I think — and am I so different from others? — I fear that having fashioned a coherent story, I have attended my own funeral. The body is in the ground, the spirit gone off on its own, and I, or someone left behind, feel empty and abandoned. Why should this happen if I had been successful in telling the truth about myself? Or had I failed to capture it each time? Was there each time a view from a parallel track that I had made use of but not recorded? I have come to think that may be so.

Each of my books, regardless of their stated intention, represents another effort to collect my working ideas, the "few familiar ideas." When I read and talk about other men, Camus, Nietzsche, I am fascinated by the problem of finding their nuclear insights. I say to myself, and to students, "If you were to name three ideas without which this man cannot be understood at all, which would they be?" Sometimes it is very difficult, sometimes the answers come easily. Sometimes we are given help, as we are by Camus, who at one time in his life was sure that experience could be summed up in nostalgia and in the absurd: "I find it hard to separate my love of light and life from my secret attachment to the experience of despair."[5] I understand what he means, but I have never had a secret attachment to despair. I understand what Nietzsche and Kafka mean too; I can even understand Sartre a good deal of the time, if I try hard. But however successfully I made their ideas mine, they are not mine as indelibly and vitally as one or two of my own. I have been nurtured by other people's ideas, but they have not made me what I am, nor can they capture me now. But I had not found myself until late in life. Every philosopher needs time to try out his ideas just as much as he needs time to experience life at different levels.

When I say "philosopher" I am not thinking of tenured members of university departments. Neither Kierkegaard nor Camus nor Marcel was such a teacher, and most of the time Nietzsche and Sartre were not either. I have in mind anyone who uses his mind to organize his experiences and his ideas into some kind of coherent structure that can help him unify his relationship to reality and at the same time make that relationship his very own. It is the business of the mind, when it is not permitted to drift, to bring order and authenticity to its vision.

The authenticity does not come from the denial or rejection of someone else's idea — except as it may make no sense — especially when it evokes recognition and sympathy. We need and we claim the wisdom of the ages; we would be desperately thin and naked, relatively helpless in our poverty, if we had our access to history and tradition cut off. One should never forget that however bent he may be, should be, on discovering the ideas that give him his special face or voice, his body as a whole will be made up of the substance of humanity and its infinite revelations and refinements. This is not a truism but a fact that towers over every obscure and modest effort to observe reality with one's own eyes.

INSECURITY AND SALVATION

The interior experience of the existential tradition is only one set of ideas that I find credible. Much within Christian experience — I do not mean the theologies that claim to be coextensive with experience — is equally and powerfully appealing to me. I could say the same of music and painting, so far as I enjoy them when I fall back on them for sympathetic reverberations after the tension of sorting out my thoughts.

I find when I have satisfied myself, after many trials and failures, that I have tended to look at myself and the world around me with two lenses, one which focuses on the insecurities of life, and my salvation, the other which looks out toward a comprehension of reality as both physical and metaphysical, one mind — body, indivisible.

Gabriel Marcel once made a dramatis persona by the name of Pascal say, "I accept absolute insecurity."[6] I have often thought about this sentence, and have concluded that I could not ever accept absolute insecurity. I do not accept any kind of insecurity, but I acknowledge each kind that I meet. I will say no more than I know, and I do not even know whether insecurity is absolute anyway. If it were, I doubt that I could accept it. But I would not let myself deny it. I respect facts, but I respect faith more, and I see no need for conflict between them. I accept a fact, and then make up my mind how to live with it. That will be my faith. If the cost of insecurity in life is vulnerability to loss of control, the cost of ignoring insecurity, of lying to oneself and others, is a constriction of experience. Whoever sees the truth and, not wanting to face it, denies it forfeits any claim to be taken seriously.

Of security one may be able to say very little at first hand. This is another fact that we ought to recognize. Many people have never known security in any form. And we need not have especially prophetic voices to cry out for them, raging against a world which permits insecurity that can be avoided. Speak boldly against insecurity, condemn it, never pass by its victims in silence. But speak tentatively when you speak of security, not carelessly. Rumors from far off reach our ears sometimes. There is security somewhere. Someone has spoken of what he has heard or seen. The blind receive their sight, the lame walk, the dead are raised, and the poor have good news preached to them. We can mention the reliable witnesses we have met. It would be preferable, of course, were we to see salvation ourselves. Many more do, I think, than even the theologians know.

The heart of insecurity is loneliness, and there is nothing more lonely than the person to whom nothing ever seems to happen. "I am the man to whom nothing ever happens" — I once said that. I had also lost confidence in the future, in a human experience in which anything can happen. The greatest discovery of my life was realizing after fifty years that I had been dead wrong. I do not say that this reversal meant that insecurity became only a memory. On the contrary, I discovered how warped I had always been by self-mistrust. The difference was that it had become possible not to be distracted by a belief that loneliness is ultimate.

The best life has to offer is to be accepted by others for what one would like to be and for what one is in spite of failure. Acceptance of this kind is the center of forgiveness or, better, of the recognition that anticipates the plea for forgiveness. We are made secure by the attention that sees into us and tells us that we are all right after all. When we find that we can count on others, we find also that they have in us someone who can be counted on in turn. To my surprise I found as I grew older that however vulnerable I felt — for reasons I could not push aside — other people increasingly depended on me, and I was able to give some of them a suggestion of security that in their worst hours they had despaired of finding again. I could do this because it had already been done for me. "We love him because he first loved us."[7] Interdependence is ultimate, not loneliness, intimacy, not isolation — to play on Camus' famous line, the mark of the human is not nostalgia but grace, the unexpected gift of self.

THE ROMANTIC THEOLOGIAN

Of course, I am now talking theological language, the science of grace, to use an unlovely but exact phrase. Theology is the science of the gifts that come true, the dreams that turn real. It is also, as Barth said, "men in their final distress and hope." Having moved from distress through and beyond hope to confidence, from *insecuritas* to *securitas*, I can appreciate now more than ever the plausibility of the theological sweep. For the first time I am willing not to duck my head when someone calls me a theologian. According to other people's standards I may not be a professional of any kind, philosopher, theologian, priest, teacher, writer. But because of my commitment to an intellectual life that requires an unrelenting exercise in the arena of interior experience, I confess that even I may be a theologian, albeit a romantic one. This may be the joker in the pack. How can a theologian, in all sobriety, be called romantic? Is not a theologian — with a nod to Barth — a receiver of God's wisdom, not a seeker? Is not the agony of the romantic alien to the piety of the man of God?

That is so, but I too have the right to bear the name because I too am dealing in ultimate weights and measures. It may be too simple a distinction to say that there are reporting theologians — who are, by the way, not much trusted these days — and romantic theologians, whose longing for presence arises out of fear and failure and is encouraged by meetings and assurances. Camus' "furious passion for life which gives meaning to all my days"[8] is so close to a definition of the theological temper that we need do no more than add "confirmed by presence." In a sense, the theologian must always be both romantic and metaphysical. He must be a passionate man and a reflective man; and he must want meaning incarnate. The word must become flesh. And so it does, all the time.

The best that life can offer is always physical as well as spiritual; the valuable is embodied coherence. We are nostalgic in all our parts; we want the whole with the whole. We want that whole to be a whole like us and to like us as the wholes we are, flawed and yet improving. Sometimes I have wondered whether Kierkegaard and Nietzsche understood such things. I am sure Pascal did not. I could wish that they had been pastors or lovers as well as thinkers. It would have made them whole men with a sane theology. The aesthetic, as Kierkegaard called the life of the senses, is not inferior; it is the skin, muscles, and guts of the spirit. Music, sun, painting, wine, and a hillside are as important to philosophy, the examination of life, and theology, the articulation of a commitment to life, as the constructs which the mind pompously leaves for posterity. We are committed to and through the whole creation, and most of all through our sensual selves, blessed, in addition to feeling, with powers of discovery and analysis.

What should a romantic theologian be capable of? First of all, experience. There is no substitute for that, and for work of any sort that brings him to know people of all kinds, and to know them well. Second, a romantic theologian should know how and when to be silent, to rest and to wait, and, while he waits, to mull over what he already has seen and thought, to stay loose so that he can listen and remember what he has heard. As the going gets tough he must learn — and it takes a long time for some of us — to control his fears and resentments so that he can at least acknowledge the power of the absurd in all its shapes without coming to believe that some kind of security is impossible. Only then is he ready to demand the truth, that is, to make demands on himself that are more insistent than those made by anyone else on him, and to attach his heart to his search for the truth of his existence so that he will be marked as a man of adoration and prayer. Finally, he must be willing to travel light, leaving aside anything that might get in his way. This he will do as he receives grace for grace, proof positive, evidence on the line, in short, the beginning of a new life.

I would say that an interior life that promises some kind of security to the romantic theologian is always centrifugal rather than centripetal. However introspective our reflection, life must be directed toward and go hand in hand with the world. Life will be receptive and dependent, and it will receive the power to teach by insight and example and to heal by means of the radiance of its own security.

Since childhood I have wanted above all a life of adventure and romance. In point of fact, I have lived an unadventurous life. My adventures have been that of the philosopher and the romantic theologian. My commitment has always been to a life in which fulfillment could come only through imagination and presence, excluding no element of mind or matter that could guarantee congruence of insight and desire. And so I say of life to life, "You are the dream I have always dreamed. You are the reality from which the dreams arose. And I am yours." For me it seems quite natural for philosophy to be superseded by theology. I do not mean that philosophy must disappear, but my guess is that it can rule safely only for an hour or so at a time and then must fade, leaving us out of breath, and that philosophy then begins again the arduous task of once more beginning at the beginning, with determination, if not always with ardor.

THE PHILOSOPHICAL IMAGINATION

It seems safe to say, we write what we know, or we ought to. But I am convinced that the most important things I have written about have been things I have not experienced. I only imagined them. And yet I knew and thought them because I could dream them. How else can I explain a preoccupation for over thirty years with the nostalgic and the lonely, the present and the withheld? I have never personally experienced tragedy. As for presence, it takes two to confirm its encounter. For the most part I have had to write out of my (philosophical, romantic?) imagination.

This is not to say that I calculated what might be and wrote that down. On the contrary, I wrote out of the depths of intense longing and conviction, never ceasing to whittle away or erase ideas. I was certain that life is both nostalgic and lonely, that we need presence above all, that the best security and satisfaction are given by presence of some kind or other. I knew that longing might be frustrated by the unexpected. I wanted to believe but always feared that there is no place, time, or person which can promise lasting security. And yet I never doubted that life is worth living only if we do not give up the nostalgia for presence.

As I now look back at the events of my life, and at my intellectual efforts, I wonder how I could have known then some of the things I only experienced later, when they seemed to be confirmations of dreams. I can recognize a slow emancipation, passing from a child's daydream to a philosopher's vision of a world groaning and travailing. I am surprised myself at the articulateness of some of these unexperienced insights.

I know that if and when my life falls apart, I shall become as numb as others who suffer indelibly. I suppose also that those who have written so convincingly about love, which is the test and paradigm of presence, probably were not always writing out of its immediacy. Perhaps this is why the most explicit descriptions of loving are those written by mystics: they live with the purity of imagination, with its intense, its exquisite experience of life as it ought to be. For mystics, what ought to be becomes and is; we are ignorant of the function of the imagination if we doubt their special validity. But for those who, while capable of being moved to some degree by the power and assurance of the mystics' imagination, nevertheless want a more translatable, a more physical response, the world we live in — and that world is essentially insecure — must be faced. One goes on living in an undependable world, waiting and working, longing and dreaming, explaining and being dissatisfied. Sustained, however, by the imagination, the only sure faculty, each of us has a right to look to a time when something of what mystics know can be realized in a world they despaired of, our mixed and tragic world of dreams and realities. The imagination is real, but not real enough. We are ultimately alone if we cannot care for and depend on someone else.

notes

preface

1. *The Politics of Experience*, p. 50.
2. *The Castle*, p. 419.
3. *The Myth of Sisyphus*, p. 198.
4. *An Augustine Synthesis*, p. 57.
5. *The Journals*, p. 171.

interior experience

1. *The Journals*, p. 303.
2. *Notebooks, 1935–1942*, p. 10.
3. Laing, *The Politics of Experience*, p. 47.

the major themes

1. EXISTENCE

1. *Unscientific Postscript*, p. 290.
2. According to Malcolm Norman (*Ludwig Wittgenstein: A Memoir*) [London: Oxford University Press, 1966], p. 71):

   > Wittgenstein once read a paper on ethics in which he said that he sometimes had a certain experience which could best be described by saying that "when I have it I wonder at the experience of the world. And then I am inclined to use such phrases as 'How extraordinary that anything should exist!' or 'How extraordinary that the world should exist!'" He went on to say that he sometimes also had "the experience of feeling absolutely safe."

   It would appear from this that Wittgenstein's intuition of existence, while similar in immediacy to that of an existentialist, vaulted over the insecurity and anguish. Not that he did not know the latter; he certainly did, but his intuition of existence was ontological — metaphysical — rather than existential (relating to his own existence). This, it seems to me, was the source of his blind spot with regard to metaphysics itself and the explanation for his reported uneasy respect for both Augustine and Kierkegaard.

3. *Being and Time*, p. 57.
4. *Existentialism*, p. 15.
5. *The Journals*, p. 46.
6. *Ibid.*, p. 235.
7. *Ibid.*, p. 15.
8. *Philosophy*, 2:4.
9. *Ibid.*, p. 5.
10. *Ibid.*, p. 4.
11. *Ibid.*, p. 3.
12. *Existentialism*, p. 18.
13. *Being and Time*, p. 68.
14. *Principles of the Philosophy of the Future*, p. 52.
15. *The Journals*, p. 315.
16. *Ibid.*, p. 51.
17. *The Innocent Voyage* [*High Wind in Jamaica*], p. 90.
18. *A Selection of His Poems and Prose*, p. 197.
19. *The Tragic Sense of Life*, p. 40.
20. *The Myth of Sisyphus*, p. 137.
21. *Notebooks, 1942–1951*, p. 81.
22. *Nausea*, p. 146.

23. *Ibid.*, p. 143.

24. *Ibid.*, p. 54.

25. *Ecce Homo,* in *The Philosophy of Nietzsche*, p. 896.

26. *The Joyful Wisdom,* in *The Portable Nietzsche*, p. 100.

27. *Ibid.*, p. 101.

28. *The Possessed*, p. 223.

29. *The Idiot*, p. 258.

30. *Ibid.*, p. 259.

31. *Notes and Counter Notes*, p. 157.

32. *Ibid.*

33. *Nausea*, p. 160; see also Kierkegaard, *The Journals*, p. 72.

34. *Nausea*, p. 84.

35. *Ibid.*, p. 98.

36. *Ibid.*, p. 129.

2. INSECURITY

1. *Confessions*, p. 17.

2. *Being and Time*, p. 335.

3. *Philosophy*, 2:177-223.

4. *Epistle to the Romans*, p. 82.

5. *Ibid.*, p. 46.

6. *Ibid.*, p. 531.

7. *The Castle*, p. 266.

8. *Pensées*, p. 37.

9. *Notebooks of Malte Laurids Brigge*, p. 17.

10. "The Death of Ivan Ilych," p. 152.

11. *Either-Or*, 2:159.

12. *Being and Having*, p. 119.

13. P. 20.

14. *Letters to Milena* [Milena Jensenska].

15. Cf. Max Brod, *Franz Kafka* (New York: Schocken Books, 1963).

16. *Letters to Milena*, p. 199.

17. *Ibid.*, p. 200.

18. *The Courage to Be*, p. 164.

3. THE VOID

1. *Pensées*, p. 66.

2. *Twilight of the Idols*, p. 483.

3. *Four Screenplays of Ingmar Bergman*, p. 112.
4. *The Joyful Wisdom*, in *The Portable Nietzsche*, p. 98.
5. *I and Thou*, passim.
6. *The Birth of Tragedy*, p. 1087; cf. E. M. Forster, "panic and emptiness" in *Howards End*.
7. *Twilight of the Idols*, pp. 485-86.
8. *The Will to Power*, p. 12.
9. *The Joyful Wisdom*, in *The Portable Nietzsche*, p. 448.
10. Letter to Franz Overbeck, February, 1883.
11. *The Possessed*, p. 636.
12. *Ibid.*, p. 637.
13. *Ibid.*, p. 112.
14. Beckett, *Waiting for Godot*, p. 52.
15. *The Words*, p. 253.
16. "Remembrance of the Poet," *Existence and Being*, p. 285.
17. *The Politics of Experience*, p. 117.
18. *Ibid.*
19. *Ibid.*, p. 136.
20. *Proust*, p. 46.
21. *Remembrance of Things Past*, 2:698.
22. *Ibid.*, p. 994.
23. *The Politics of Experience*, p. 32.

4. SELF-ISOLATION

1. *Confessions*, p. 84.
2. *Ibid.*, p. 75.
3. *Ibid.*, pp. 217-27.
4. *An Augustine Synthesis*, p. 422.
5. *Ibid.*
6. *Confessions*, p. 51.
7. *Ibid.*
8. *Epistle to the Romans*, chap. 7.
9. *The Brothers Karamazov*, p. 683.
10. *Ibid.*, p. 356.
11. *Ibid.*, p. 911.
12. *The Divided Self*, p. 38.
13. *The Politics of Experience*, p. 47.
14. *Sickness unto Death*, p. 89.
15. *Ibid.*, p. 100.

16. *The Possessed*, pp. 690–91.
17. *Letter to His Father*, p. 73.
18. *The Great Wall of China*, p. 264; cf. also Wittgenstein's parable about philosophy, as reported by Norman Malcolm in *Wittgenstein: A Memoir*, p. 51: "A person caught in a philosophical confusion is like a man in a room who wants to get out but doesn't know how. He tries the window but it is too high. He tries the chimney but it is too narrow. And if he would only turn around, he would see that the door has been open all the time!"
19. *Letter to His Father*, p. 89.
20. *Ibid.*, p. 113.
21. In the spirit of Kafka, Laing has written (*Knots*, p. 85):

> Before one goes through the gate
> one may not be aware there is a gate
> One may think there is a gate to go through
> and look a long time for it
> without finding it
> One may find it and
> it may not open
> If it opens one may be through it
> As one goes through it
> One sees that the gate one went through
> was the self that went through it.

22. *Existential Psychoanalysis*, p. 153.
23. *Ibid.*
24. *Being and Nothingness*, passim.
25. *Existential Psychoanalysis*, p. 152.
26. *Being and Nothingness*, pt. 3, chap. 3, passim.
27. *The Divided Self*, chap. 6.
28. *Existential Psychoanalysis*, p. 209.
29. *Confessions*, p. 81.
30. *Ibid.*, p. 111.
31. *Ibid.*, p. 60.

5. PRESENCE

1. *I and Thou*, p. 18.
2. *The Politics of Experience*, p. 117.
3. Cf. *ibid.*, p. 15.

4. *Pensées*, p. 49.

5. *Ibid.*

6. *Remembrance of Things Past*, 2:996.

7. *Ibid.*

8. *Ibid.*

9. *Ibid.*

10. *Ibid.*, p. 995.

11. *I and Thou*, p. 6.

12. "On the Ontological Mystery," in *The Philosophy of Existence*, p. 27.

13. *I and Thou*, p. 95.

14. *The Divided Self*, p. 113.

15. *The Mystery of Being*, 1:205.

16. *The Politics of Experience*, p. 153.

17. *Waiting for God*, p. 44.

18. *Song of Songs*, chaps. 7, 1.

19. Cf. André Malraux's passage on ecstasy in *Man's Fate* (New York: Vintage Books, 1961): "I'm looking for a word stronger than joy. There is no word. . . . Nearer what you call . . . ecstasy. Yes. But thick. Deep. Not light. An ecstasy towards . . . downwards" (p. 147). What is usually called ecstasy is not only brief, it is an experience of isolation. What Malraux has in mind is a satisfaction experienced in final union, one that spreads itself all over and through. Mystical or sexual, the description would be the same. Perhaps it is the final mark of presence, the one without a name.

afterword: A VIEW FROM A PARALLEL TRACK

1. *The Blue and Brown Books*, p. 45.

2. Quoted in Malcolm, *Wittgenstein: A Memoir*, p. 100.

3. *The Myth of Sisyphus*, p. 198.

4. *Lyrical and Critical Essays*, p. 76.

5. *Ibid.*, p. 51.

6. *Rome n'est plus dans Rome* (Paris: La Table Ronde, 1951), p. 146.

7. 1 John 4:19.

8. *Notebooks, 1935–42*, p. 58.

bibliography

This is a selected bibliography, made up of works cited in the text or otherwise used in its preparation. The selection and its chronological sequence are intended to suggest the scope of the existential tradition.

The Jerusalem Bible. New York: Doubleday, 1966.
St. Augustine. *Confessions*. Translated by Rex Warner. New York: New American Library, 1963.
_____. *An Augustine Synthesis*. Arranged by Erich Przywara. New York: Harper, 1958.
Pascal, Blaise. *Pensées*. Introduction by T. S. Eliot. New York: E. P. Dutton, 1954.
Kierkegaard, Sören. *Either-Or*. Princeton: Princeton University Press, 1949.

_____. *Sickness unto Death*. Princeton: Princeton University Press, 1944.

_____. *Unscientific Postscript to the Philosophical Fragments*. Princeton: Princeton University Press, 1941.

_____. *The Journals*. New York: Oxford University Press, 1951.

Feuerbach, Ludwig. *Principles of the Philosophy of the Future*. New York: Bobbs-Merrill, 1966.

_____. *The Essence of Christianity*. New York: Harper, 1957.

Tolstoy, Leo. "The Death of Ivan Ilych." In *The Death of Ivan Ilych and Other Stories*. New York: New American Library, 1960.

Dostoevsky, Fyodor. *Letters from the Underworld*. New York: E. P. Dutton, 1953.

_____. *Crime and Punishment*. New York: Heritage Press, 1938.

_____. *The Possessed*. New York: New American Library, 1962.

The Brothers Karamazov. New York: Penguin Books, 1958.

_____. *The Idiot*. Baltimore: Penguin Books, 1955.

Nietzsche, Friederich. *The Birth of Tragedy*. In *The Philosophy of Nietzsche*. New York: Modern Library, 1927.

_____. *The Joyful Wisdom*. London: T. N. Foulis, 1910.

_____. *Twilight of the Idols*. In *The Portable Nietzsche*. New York: Viking Press, 1954.

_____. *The Will to Power*. New York: Random House, 1967.

Gerard Manley Hopkins. *A Selection of His Poems and Prose*. Baltimore: Penguin Books, 1962.

Unamuno, Miguel de. *The Tragic Sense of Life*. New York: Dover Publications, 1954.

Kafka, Franz. *The Trial*. New York: Modern Library, 1956.

_____. *The Castle*. New York: Alfred A. Knopf, 1956.

_____. *The Great Wall of China*. New York: Schocken Books, 1946.

_____. *Letters to Milena*. New York: Schocken Books, 1953.

_____. *Letter to His Father*. New York: Schocken Books, 1966.

Proust, Marcel. *Remembrance of Things Past*. New York: Random House, 1934.

Rilke, Rainer Maria. *The Notebooks of Malte Laurids Brigge*. New York: W. W. Norton, 1949.

Barth, Karl. *The Epistle to the Romans*. London: Oxford University Press, 1953.

Jaspers, Karl. *Philosophy*. Vol. 2. Chicago: University of Chicago Press, 1970.

Buber, Martin. *I and Thou*. New York: Charles Scribner's Sons, 1958.

Heidegger, Martin. *Being and Time*. New York: Harper and Row, 1962.

_____. *Existence and Being*. Chicago: Henry Regnery, 1949.

Marcel, Gabriel. *Being and Having*. London: Dacre Press, London, 1949.

_____. *The Philosophy of Existence*. London: Harvill Press, 1954.

_____. *The Mystery of Being*. Vol. 1. London: Harvill Press, 1950.

Tillich, Paul. *Systematic Theology*. 2 vols. Chicago: University of Chicago Press, 1951-57.

_____. *The Courage to Be*. New Haven: Yale University Press, 1952.

Sartre, Jean-Paul. *Being and Nothingness*. New York: Citadel Press, 1966.

_____. *Existentialism*. New York: Philosophical Library, 1947.

_____. *Nausea*. New York: New Directions, 1964.

_____. *Existential Psychoanalysis*. Chicago: Henry Regnery, 1967.

_____. *The Words*. New York: George Braziller, 1964.

Weil, Simone. *Waiting for God*. New York: G. P. Putnam, 1951.

Wittgenstein, Ludwig. *Tractatus Logico-Philosophicus*. London: Routledge and Kegan Paul, 1961.

_____. *The Blue and Brown Books*. New York: Harper and Row, 1965.

_____. *Philosophical Investigations*. Oxford: Basil Blackwell, 1967.

Camus, Albert. *The Myth of Sisyphus*. New York: Alfred A. Knopf, 1951.

159 § bibliography

_____. *Notebooks, 1935-42*. New York: Alfred A. Knopf, 1969.

_____. *Notebooks, 1942-51*. New York: Modern Library, 1965.

_____. *The Rebel*. New York: Alfred A. Knopf, 1964.

_____. *Lyrical and Critical Essays*. New York: Alfred A. Knopf, 1969.

Goldmann, Lucien. *The Hidden God*. New York: Humanities Press, 1964.

Beckett, Samuel. *Waiting for Godot*. New York: Grove Press, 1954.

_____. *Proust*. New York: Grove Press, 1931.

_____. *Krapp's Last Tape*. New York: Grove Press, 1960.

Ionesco, Eugene. *Notes and Counter Notes*. New York: Grove Press, 1964.

_____. *Hunger and Thirst*. New York: Grove Press, 1969.

_____. *The Killer*. New York: Grove Press, 1960.

Bergman, Ingmar. *Four Screenplays of Ingmar Bergman*. New York: Simon and Schuster, 1960.

_____. *A Film Trilogy*. New York: Orion Press, 1967.

Pinter, Harold. *The Birthday Party*. New York: Grove Press, 1968.

_____. *The Homecoming*. New York: Grove Press, 1966.

_____. *Landscape and Silence*. London: Methuen Co., 1969.

Laing, R. D. *The Divided Self*. Baltimore: Penguin Books, 1967.

_____. *The Politics of Experience*. Baltimore: Penguin Books, 1969.

_____. *Knots*. New York: Pantheon Books, 1970.

index

This book was composed in Highland text and Stettler display type
by Jones Composition Company from a design by Victoria Dudley.
It was printed by The Murray Printing Company on S. D. Warren's 60-lb.
Sebago paper, in a text shade, regular finish. The cloth edition
was bound by Moore and Company in Columbia Mills' Llamique.
The paperback edition was bound by The Murray Printing Company.

Library of Congress Cataloging in Publication Data

Harper, Ralph, 1915—
The existential experience.

Bibliography: p.
1. Existentialism. 2. Experience. I. Title.

B819.H298   142'.7   72-4009
ISBN 0-8018-1409-X
ISBN 0-8018-1423-5 (pbk.)